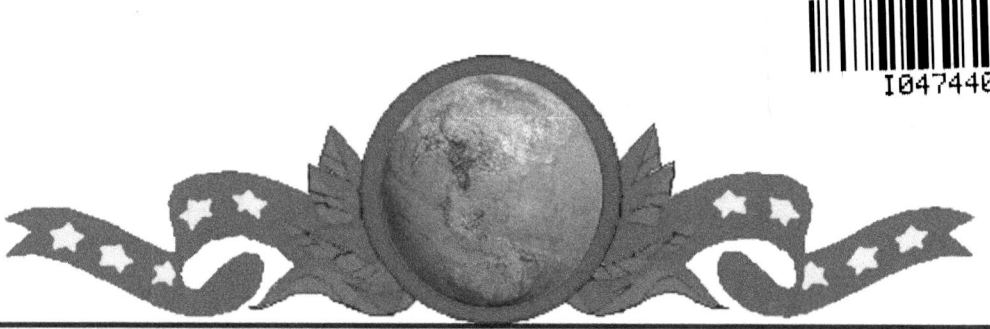

Real World
Colouring Book
For Advanced Users & Adults

Copyright 2019 By John Boom

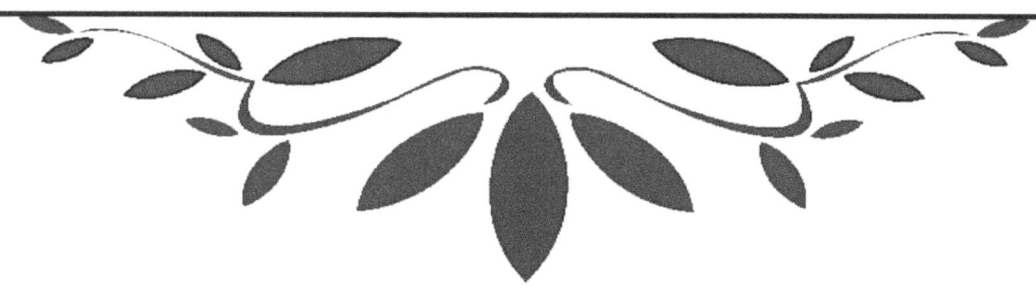

50 Images

Created From Real Life Photos
For You To Colour As You Please.

ISBN 978-0-359-93599-4

90000

9 780359 935994

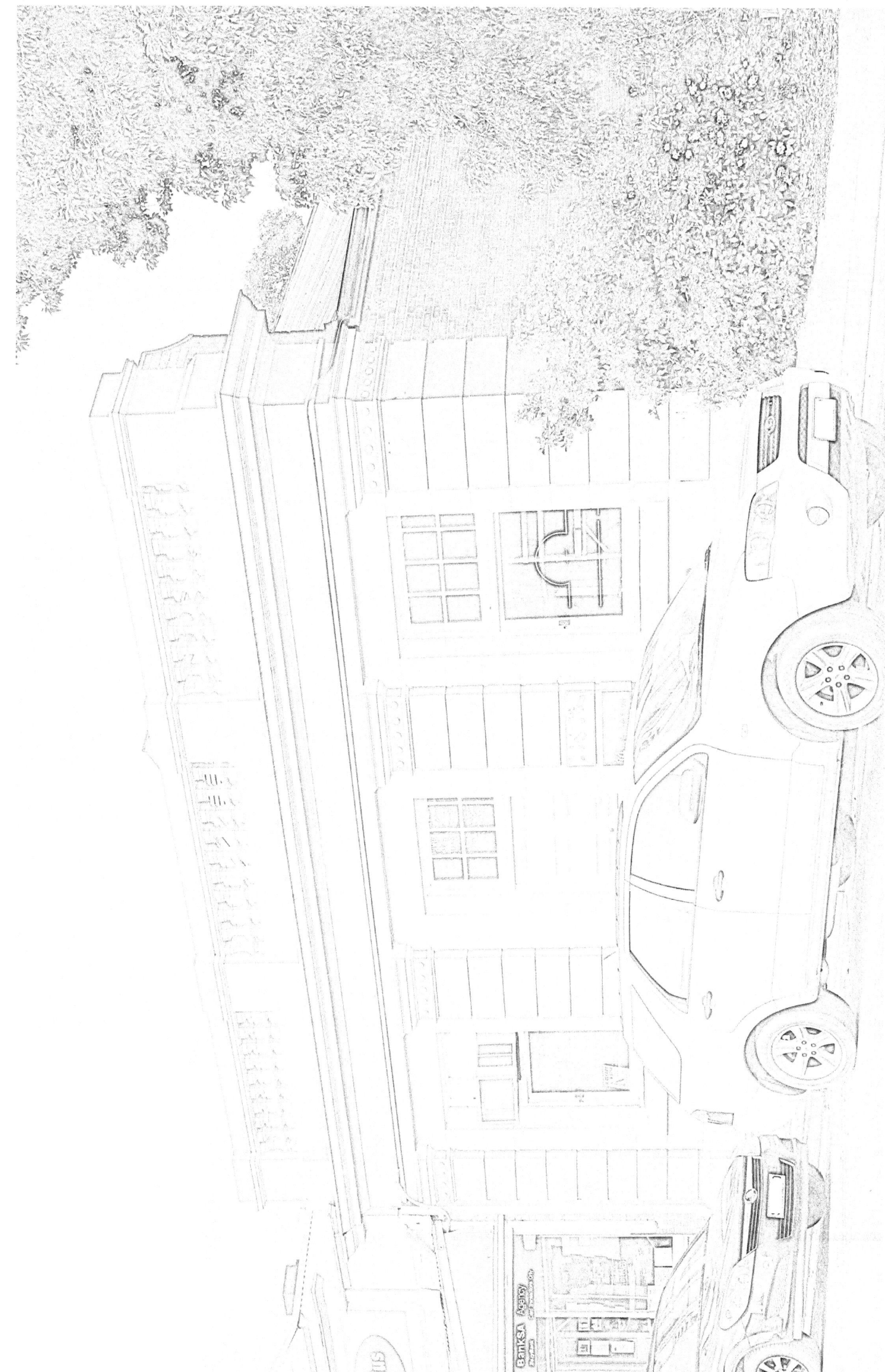

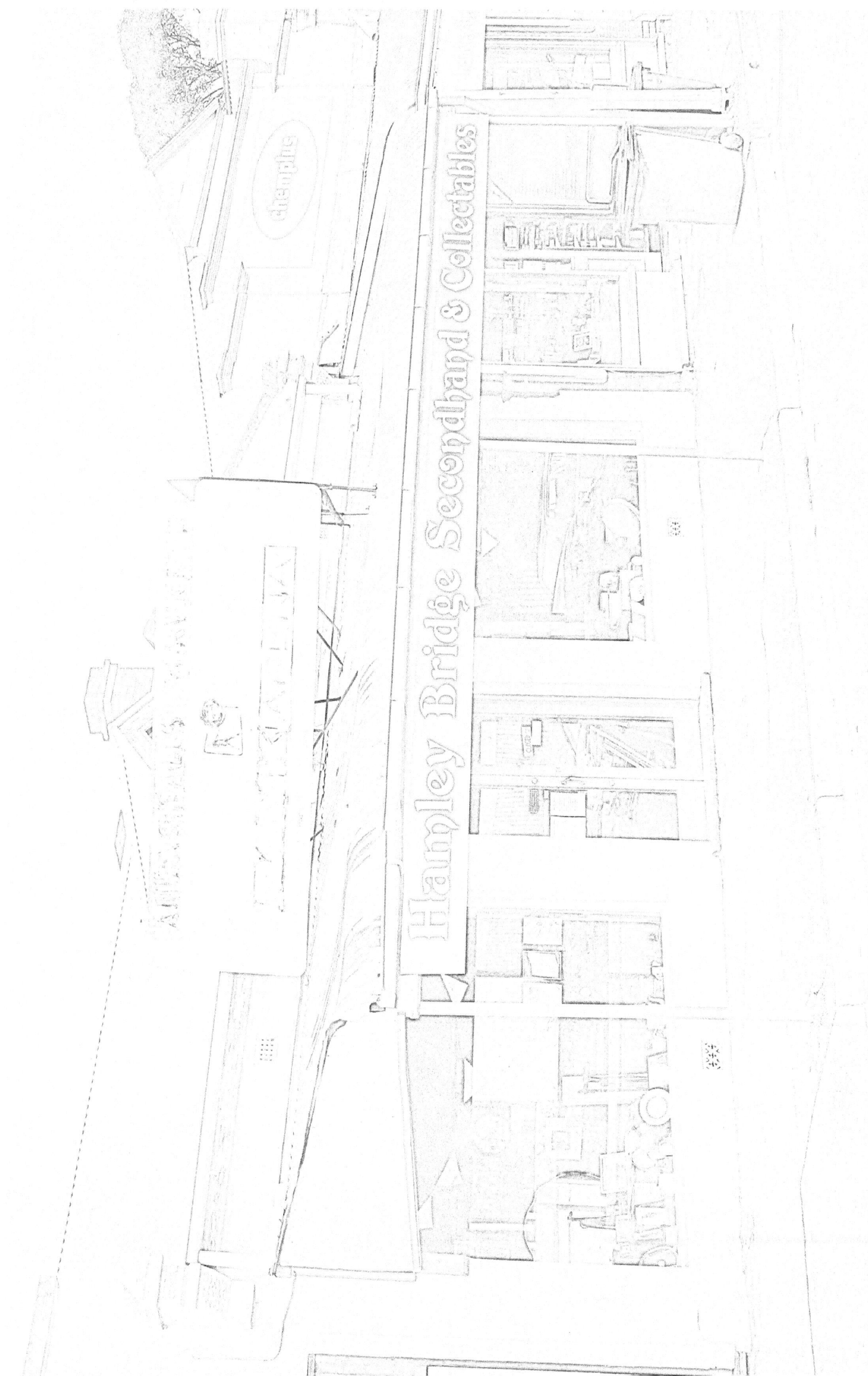

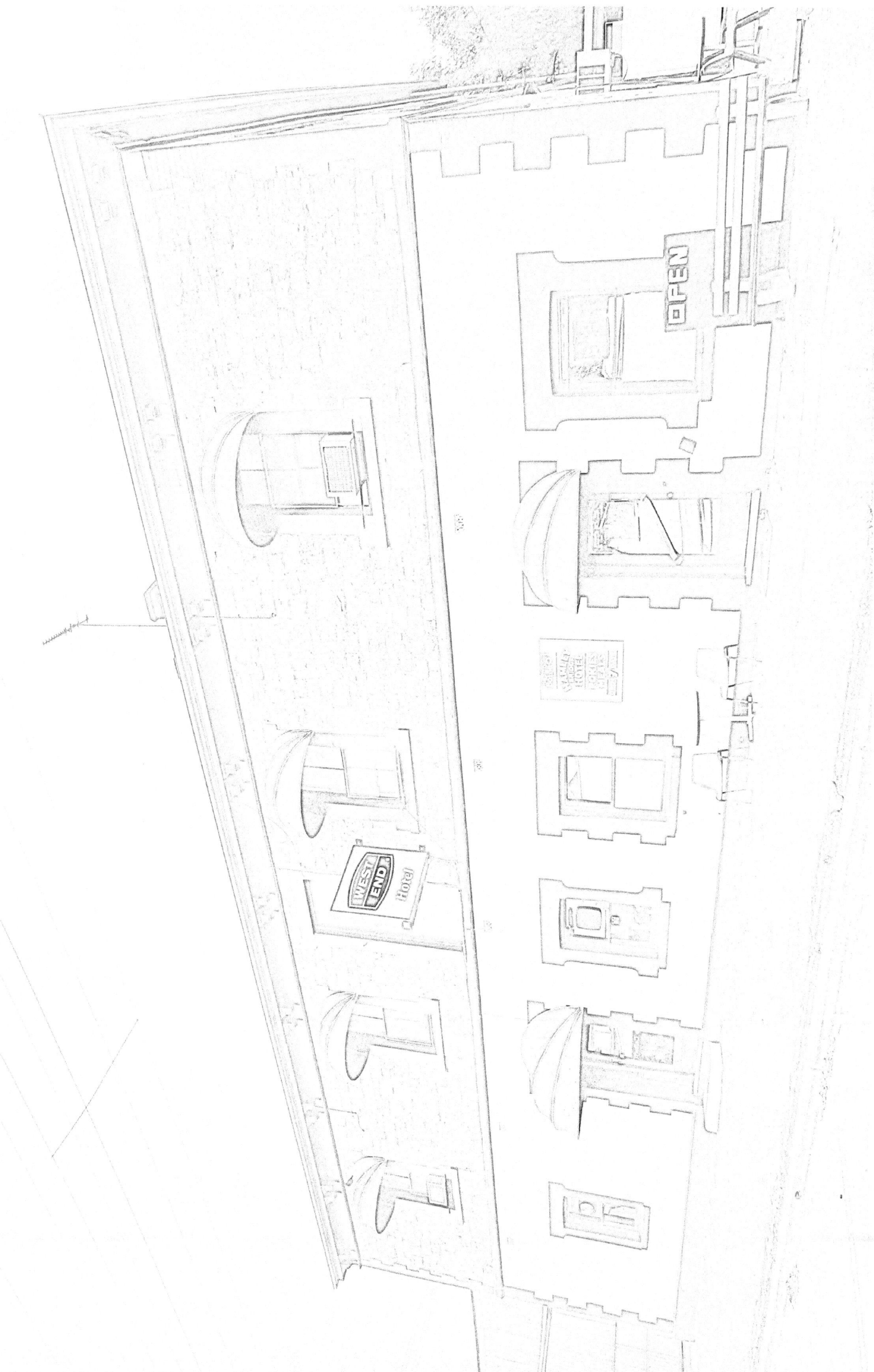

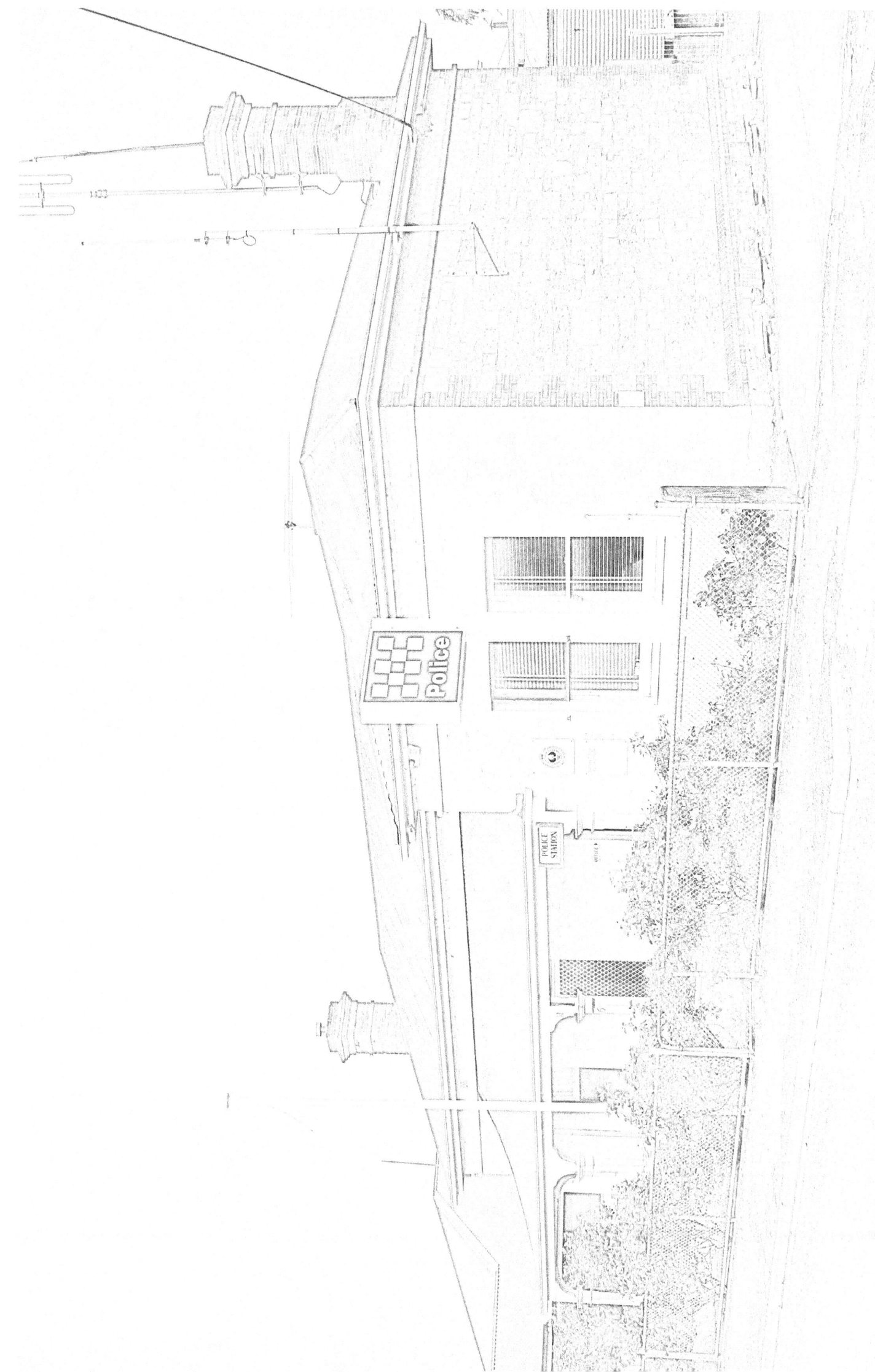

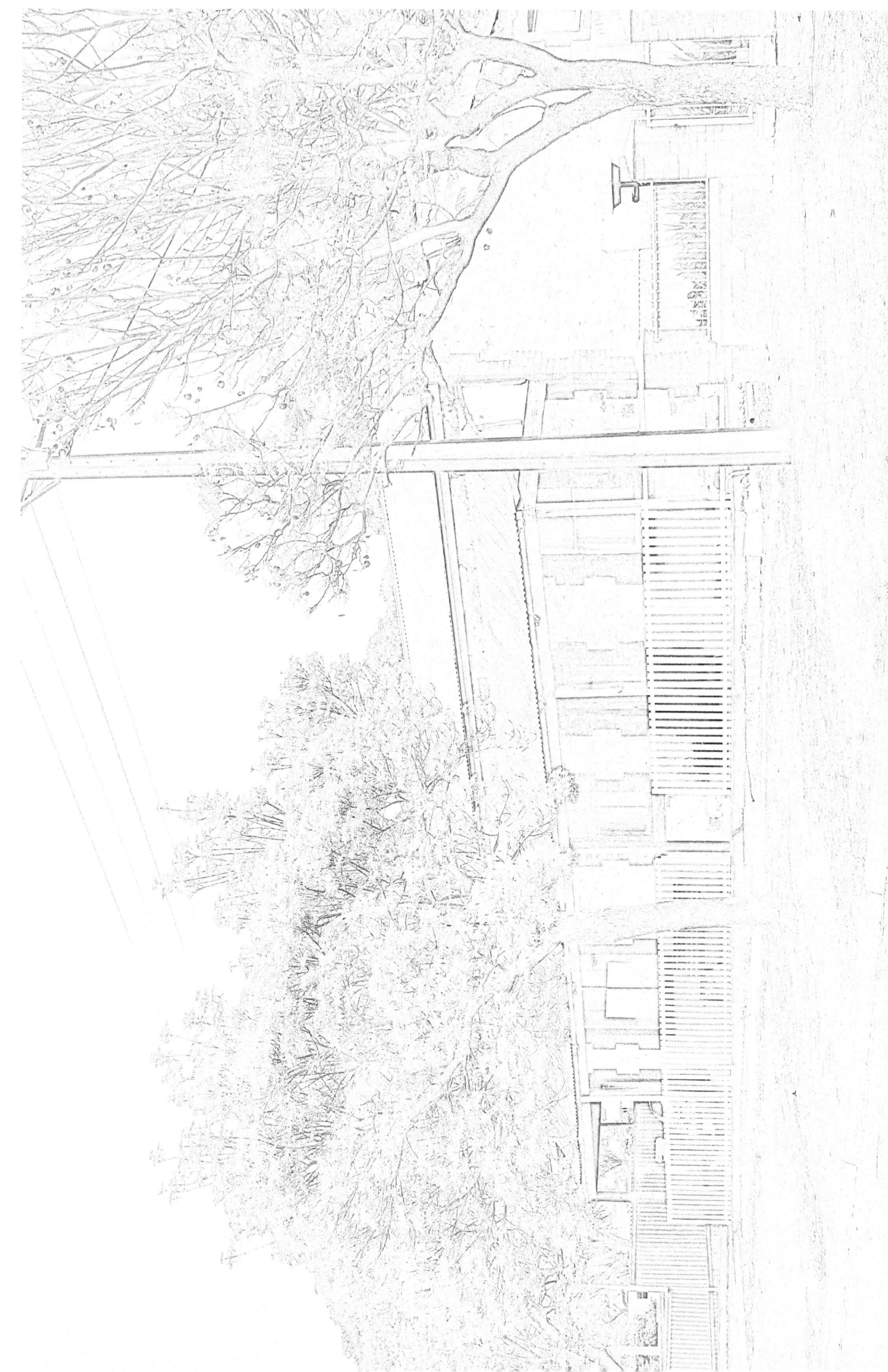

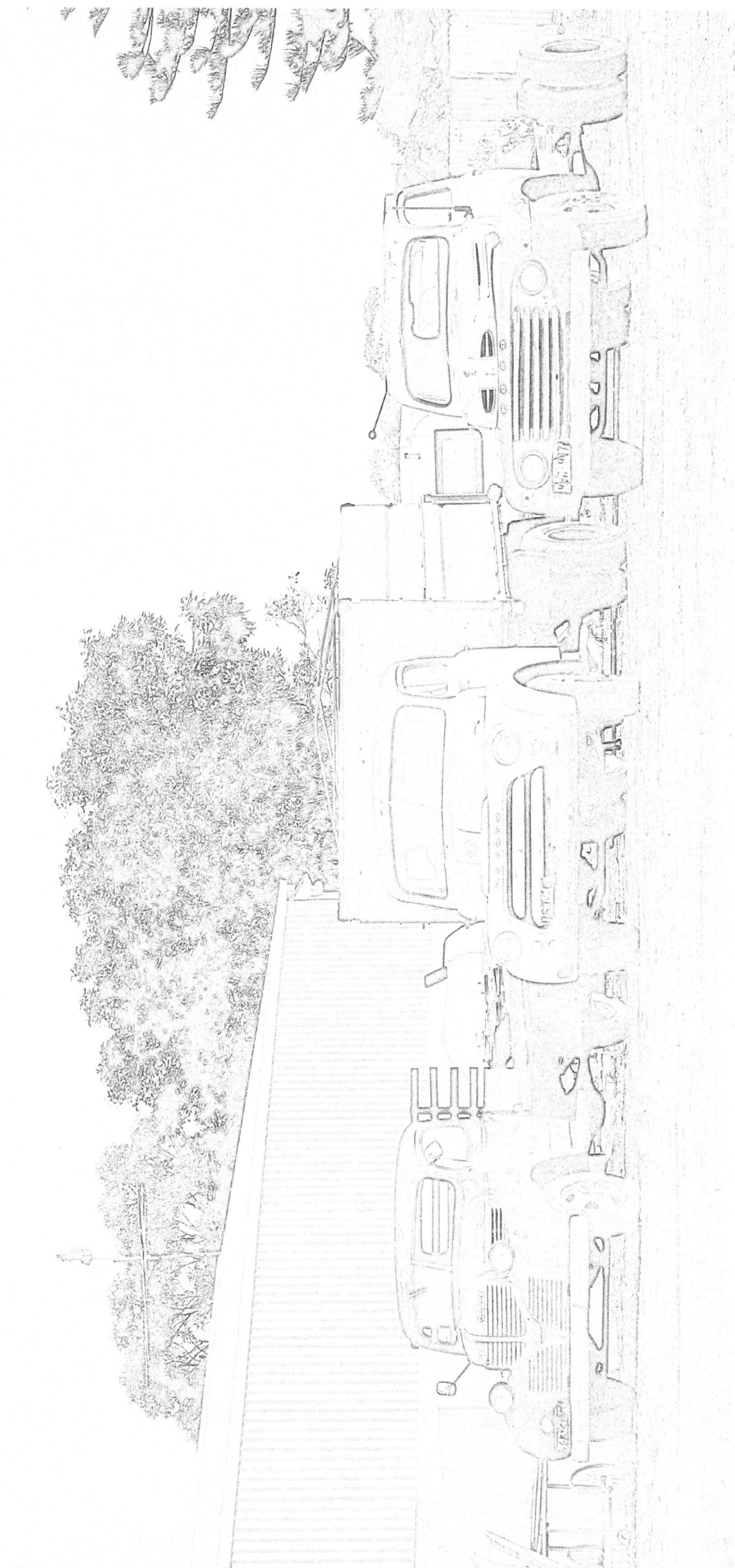

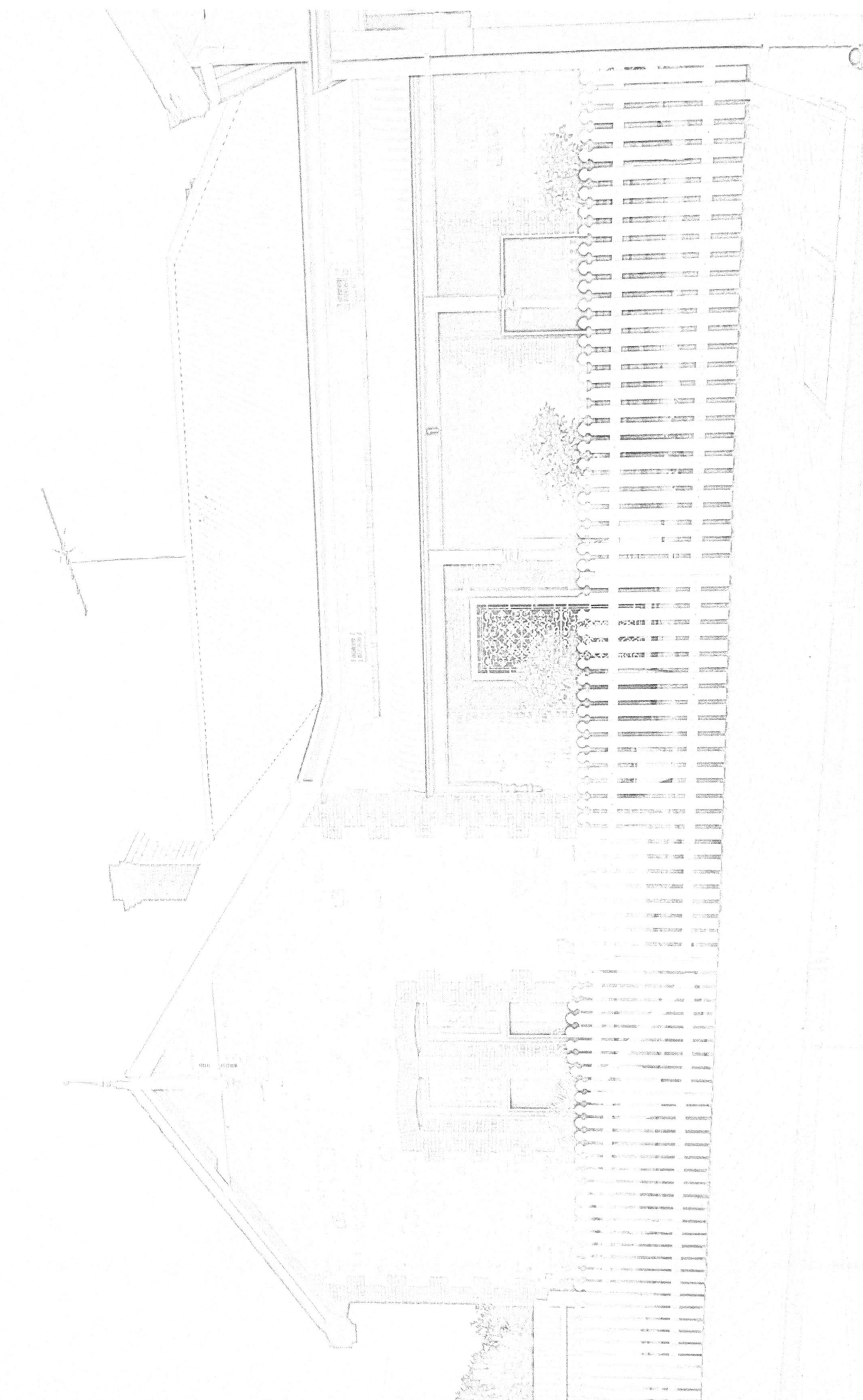

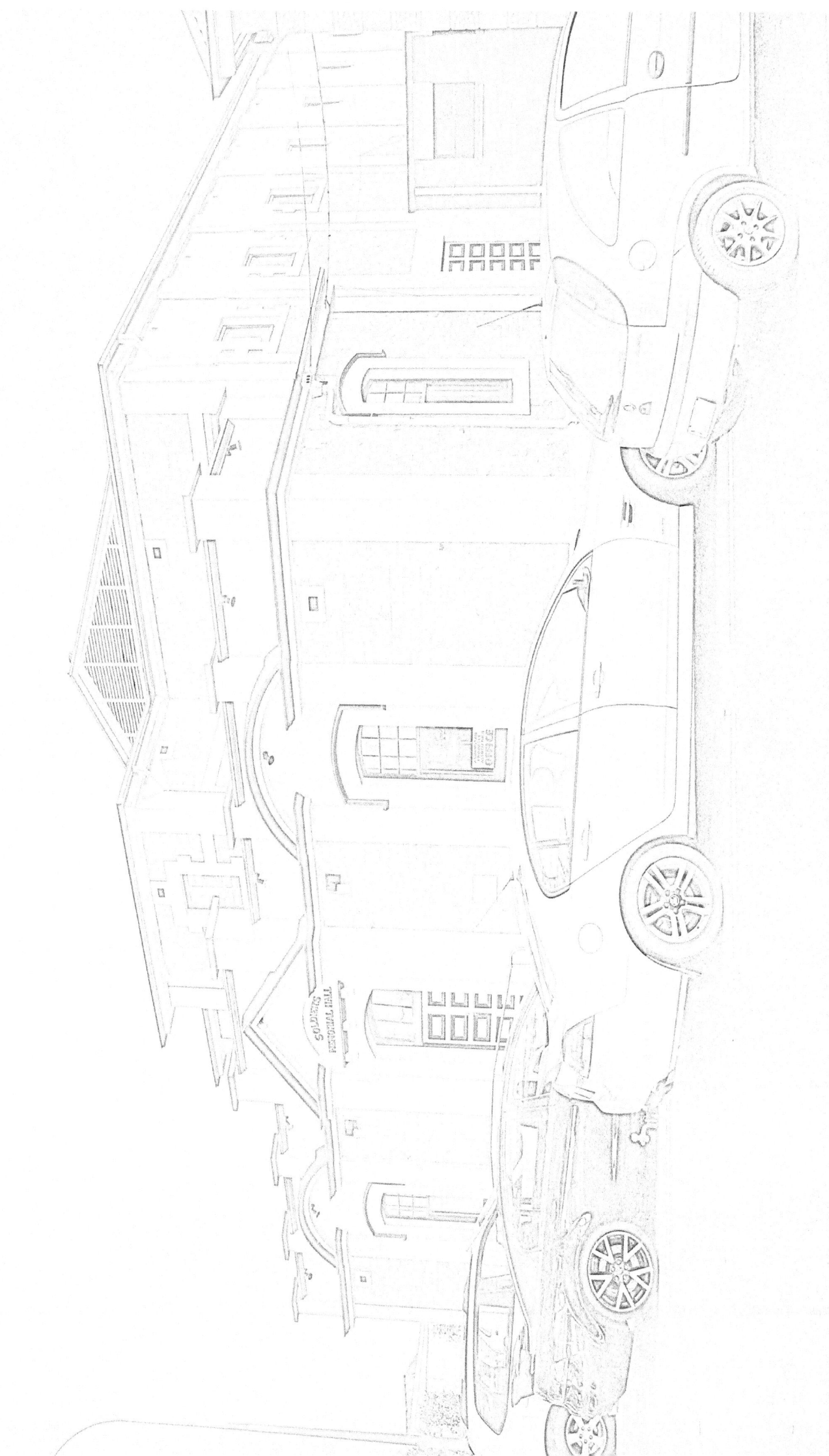

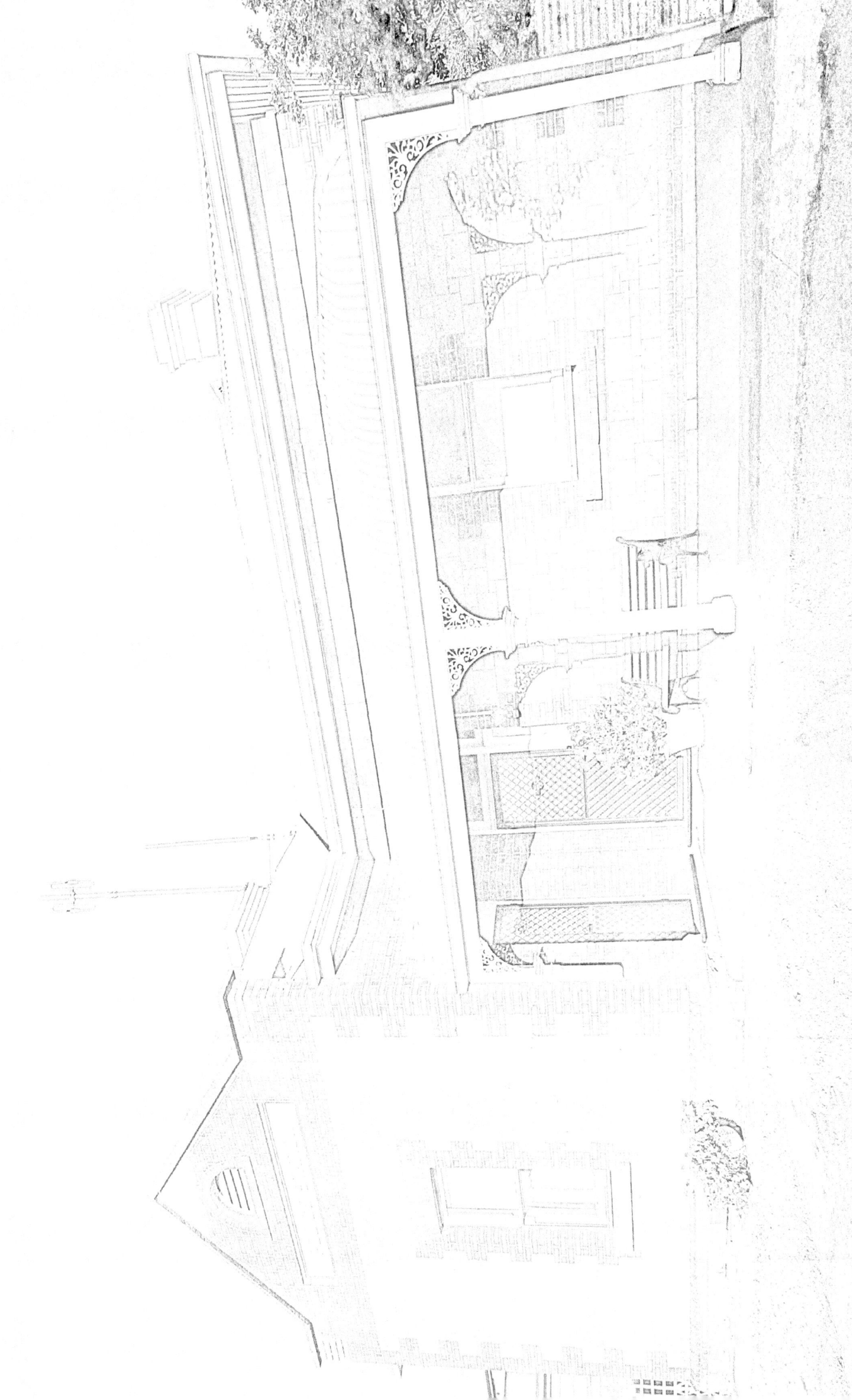

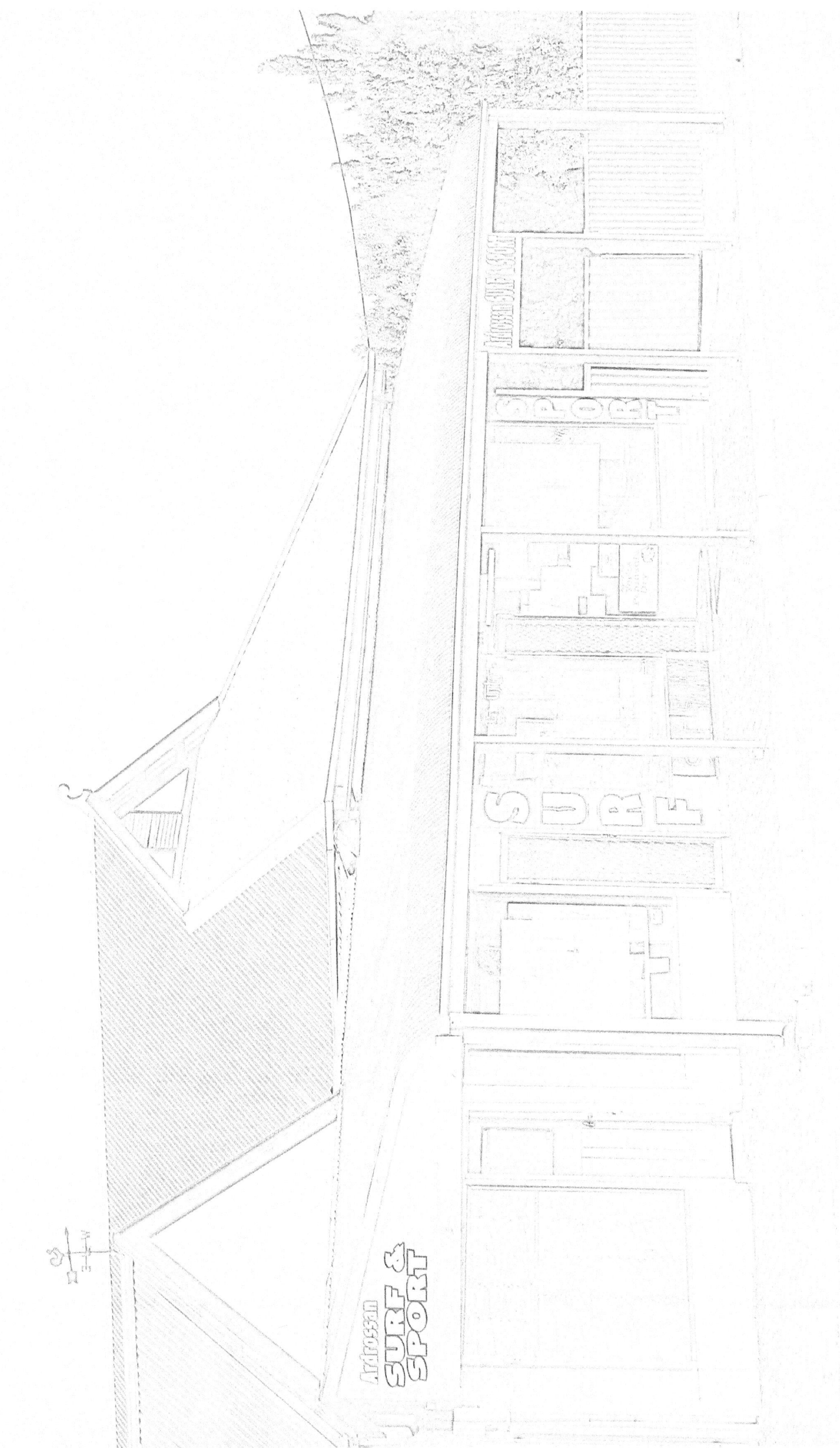

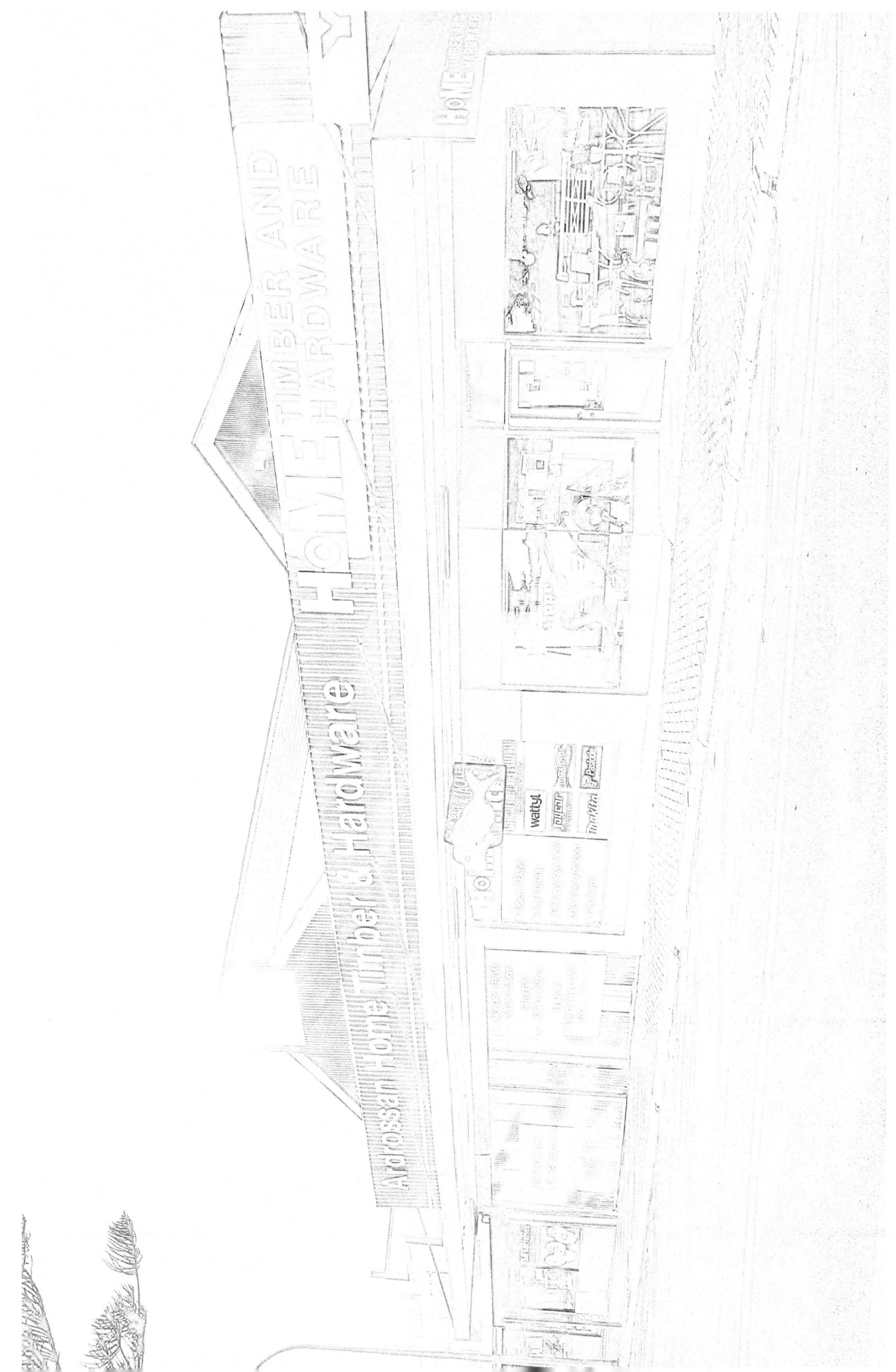

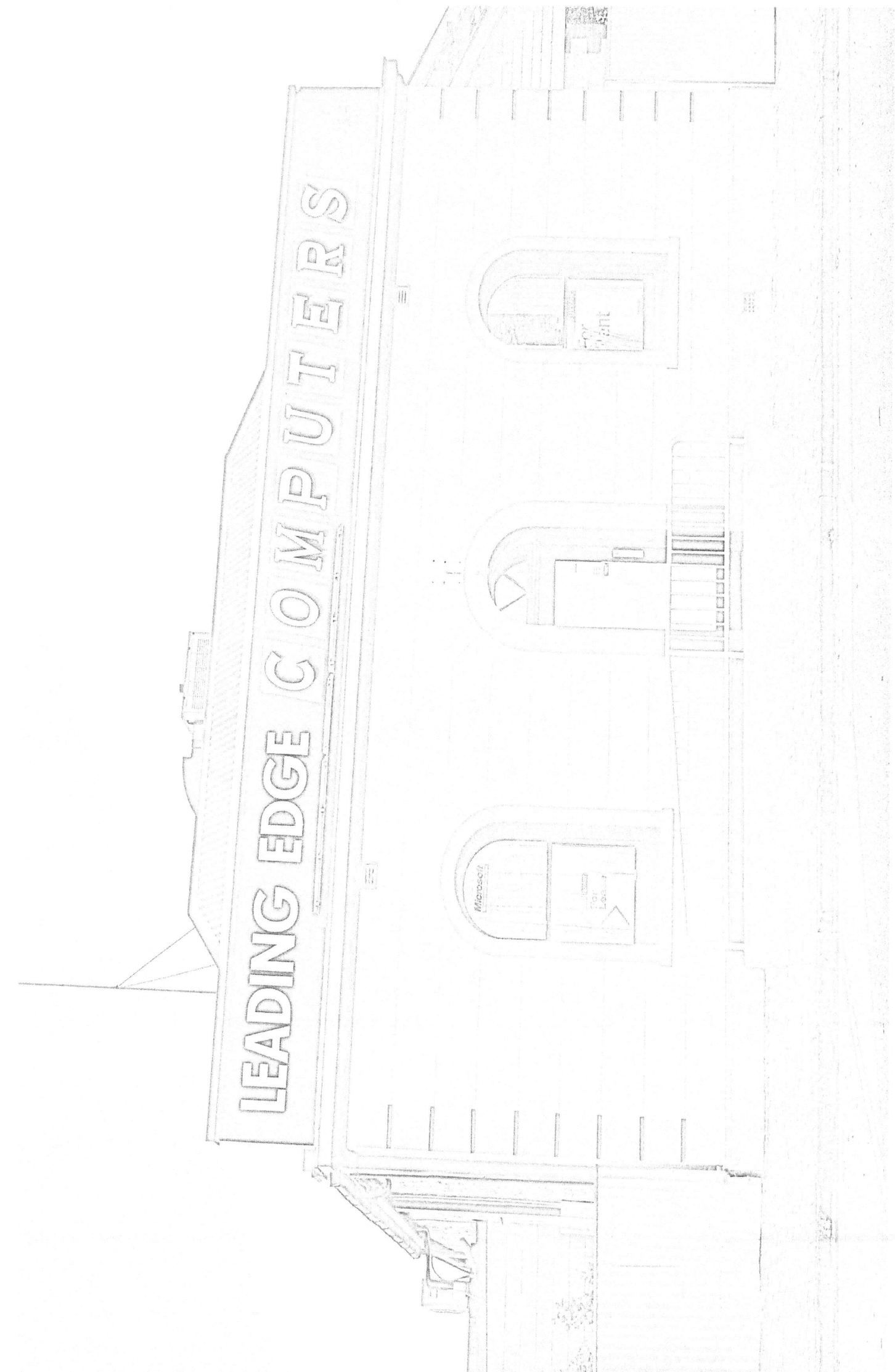

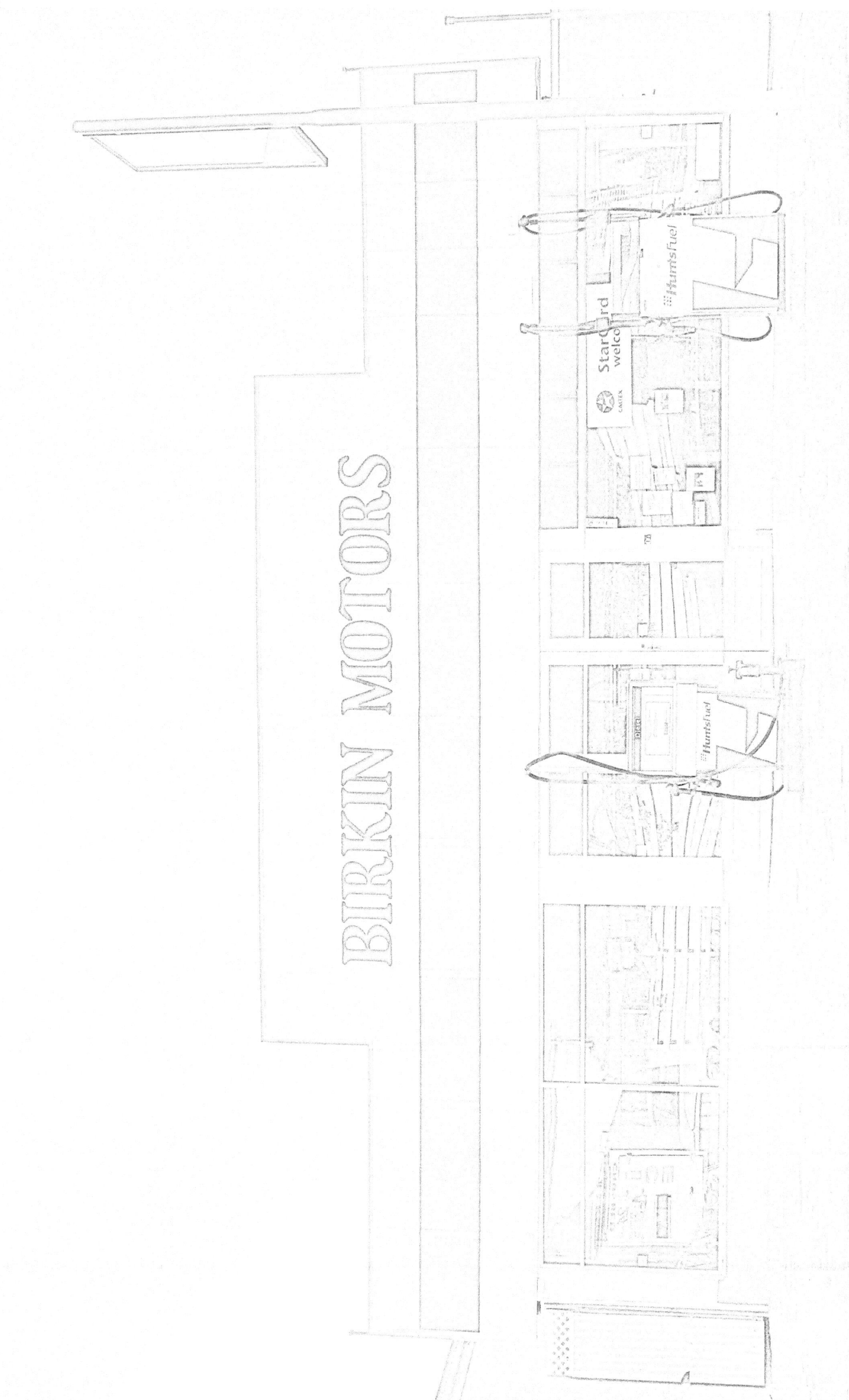

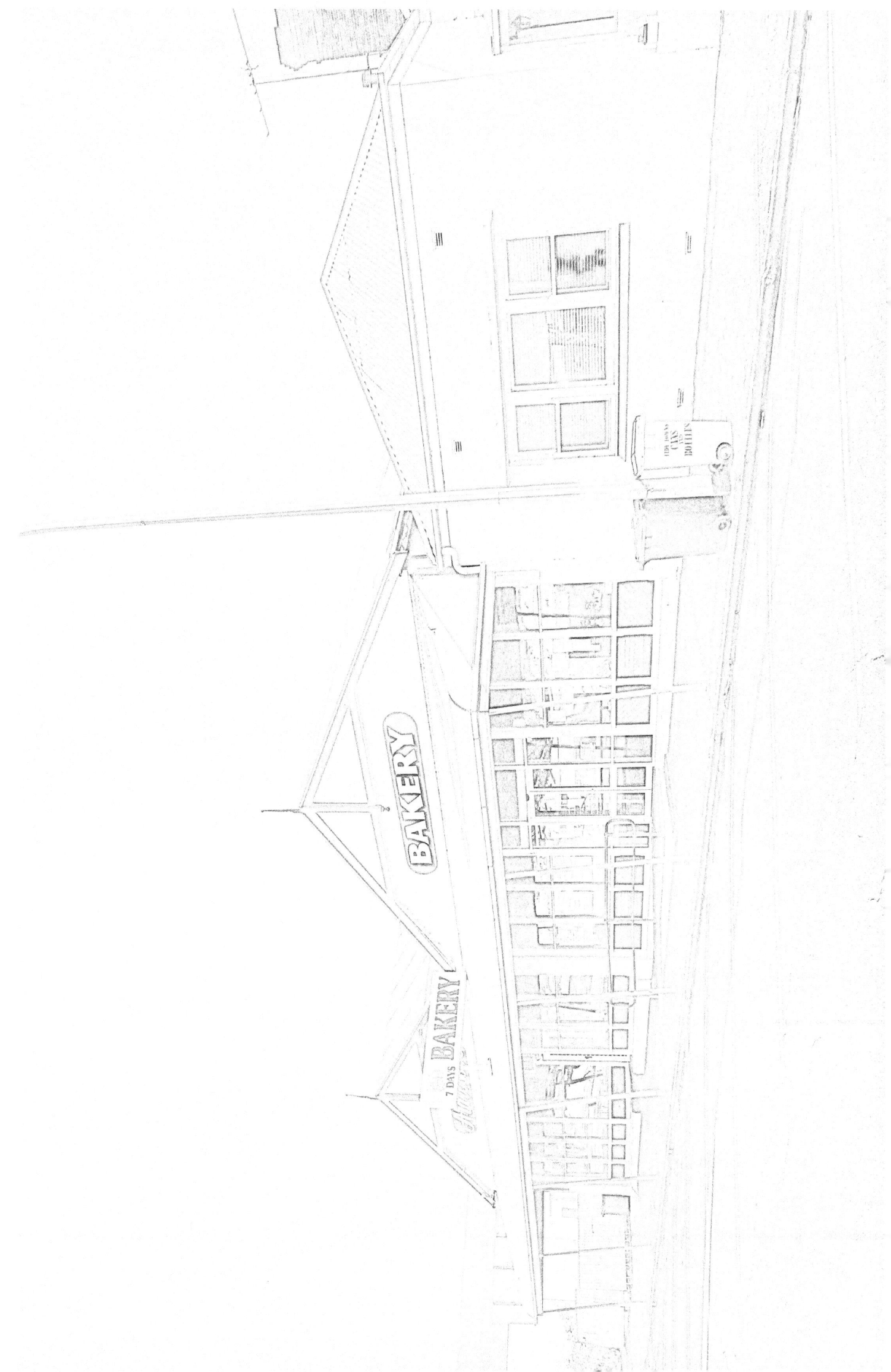

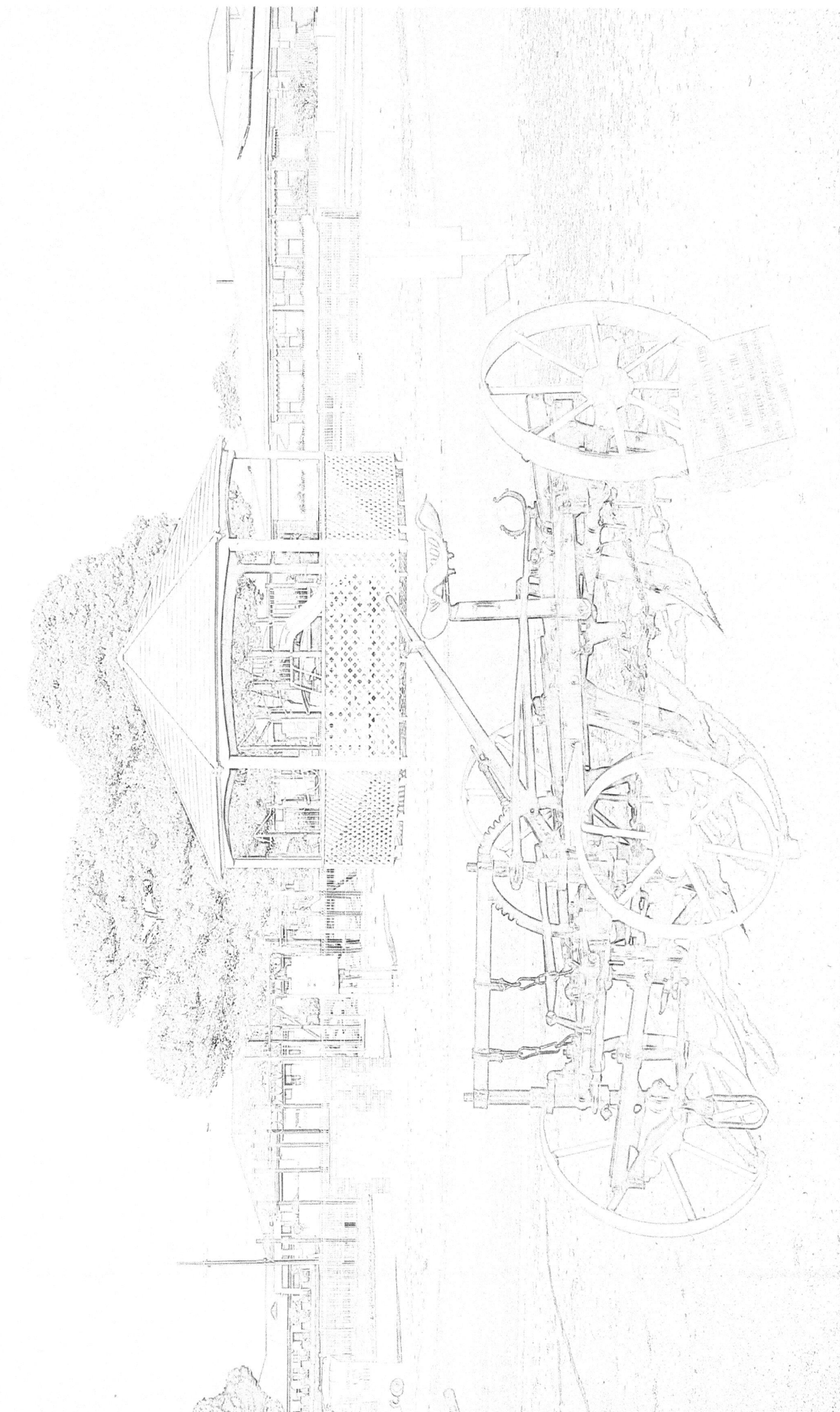

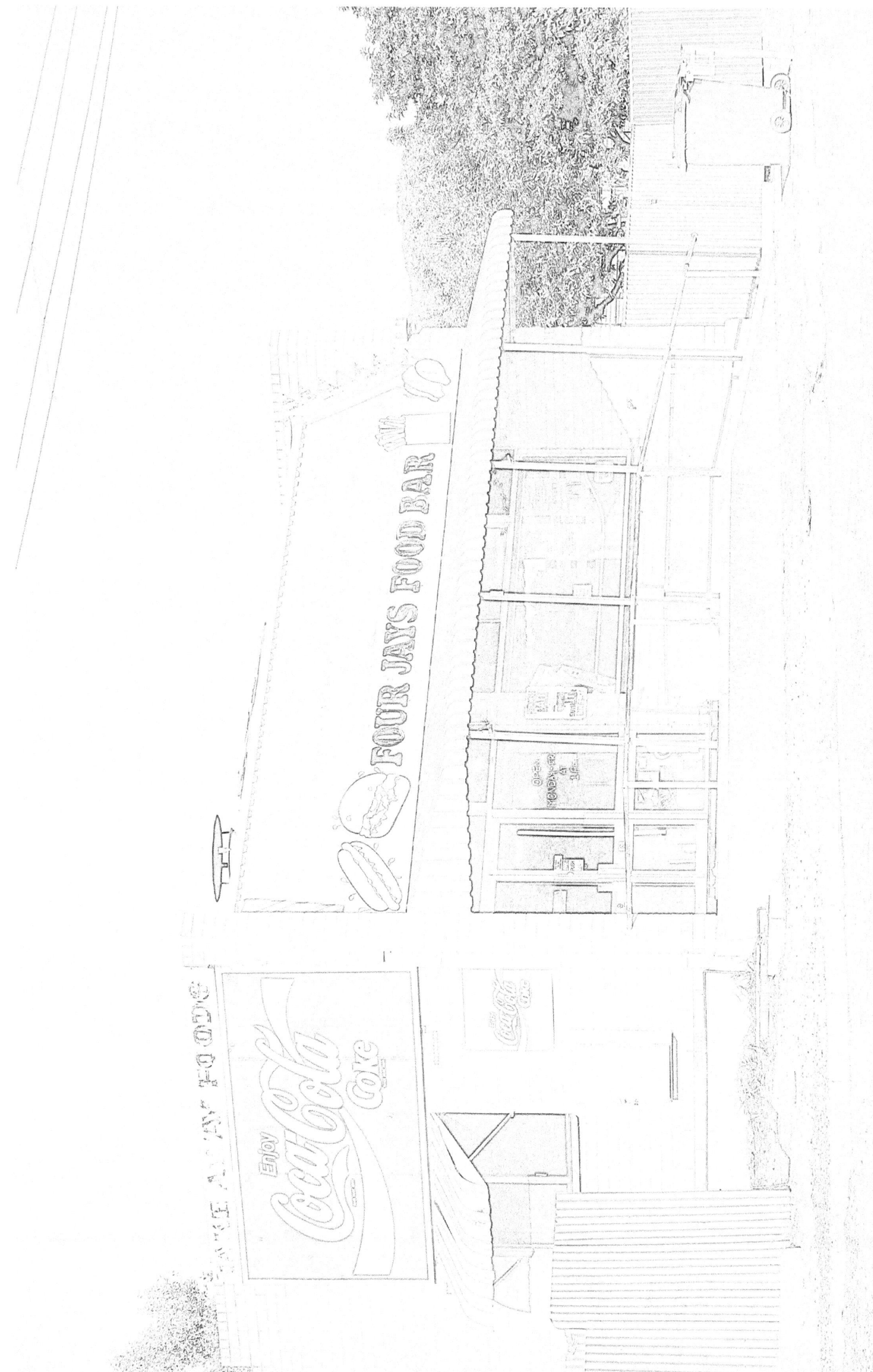

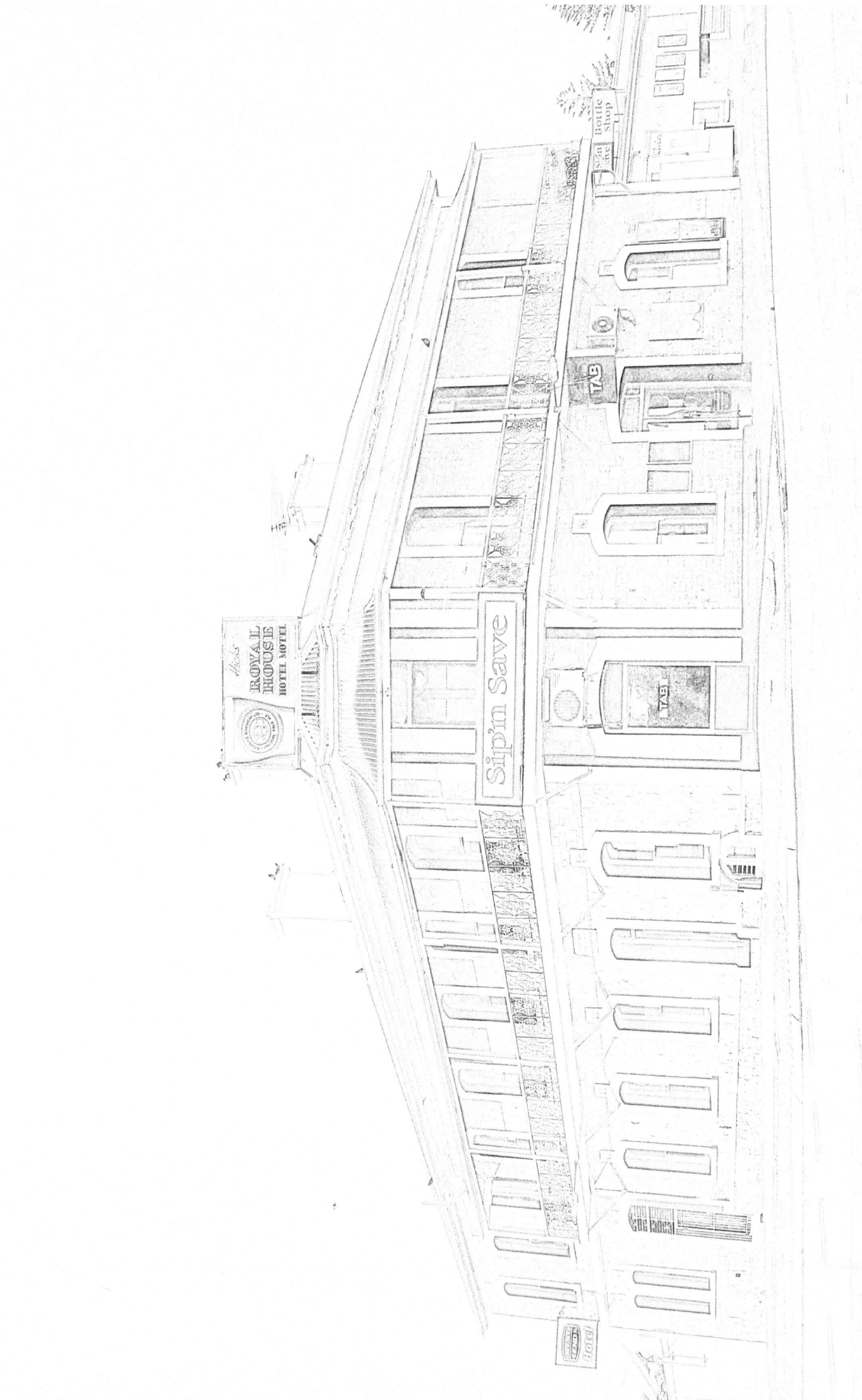

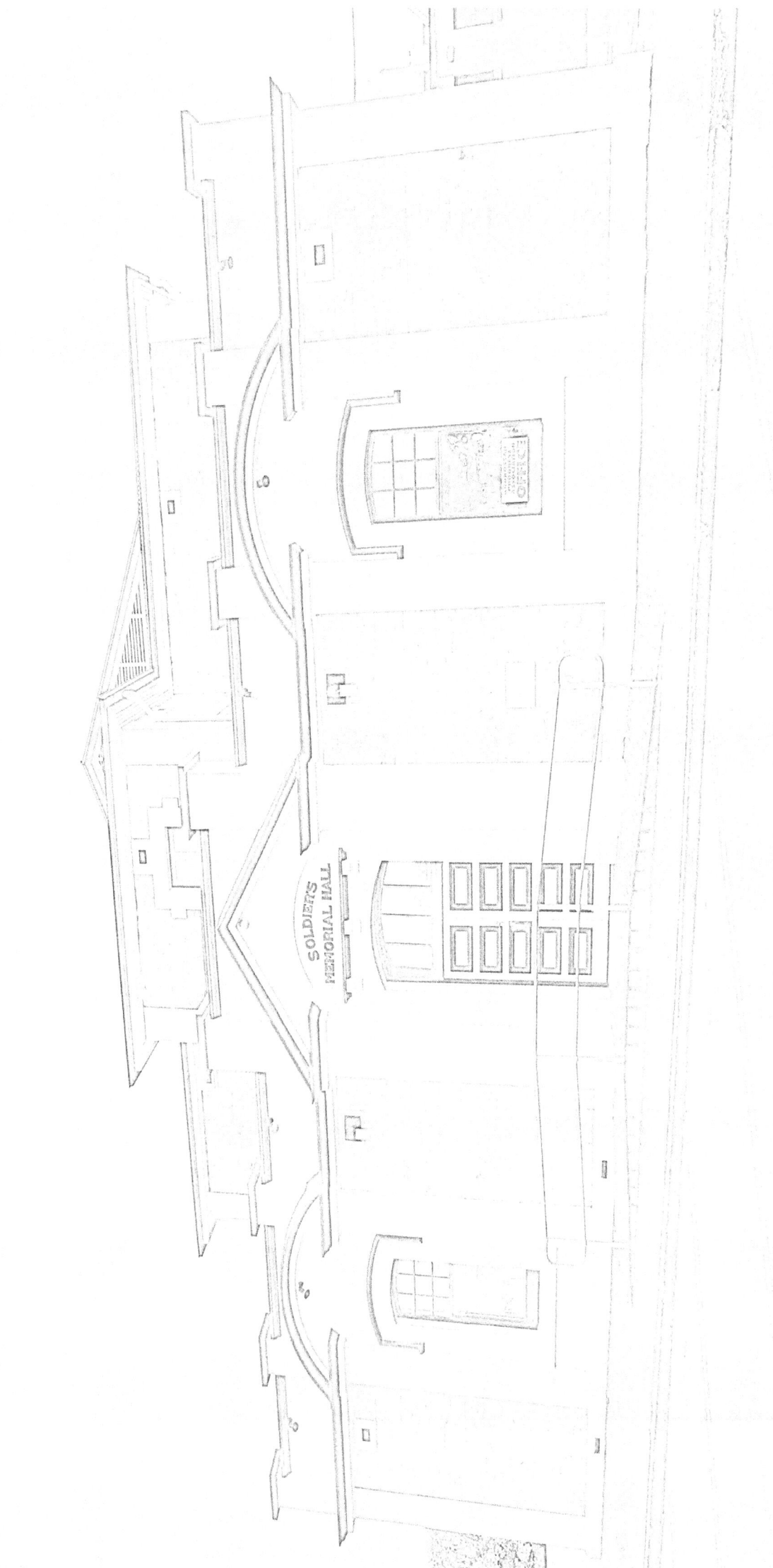

SOLDIERS
MEMORIAL HALL

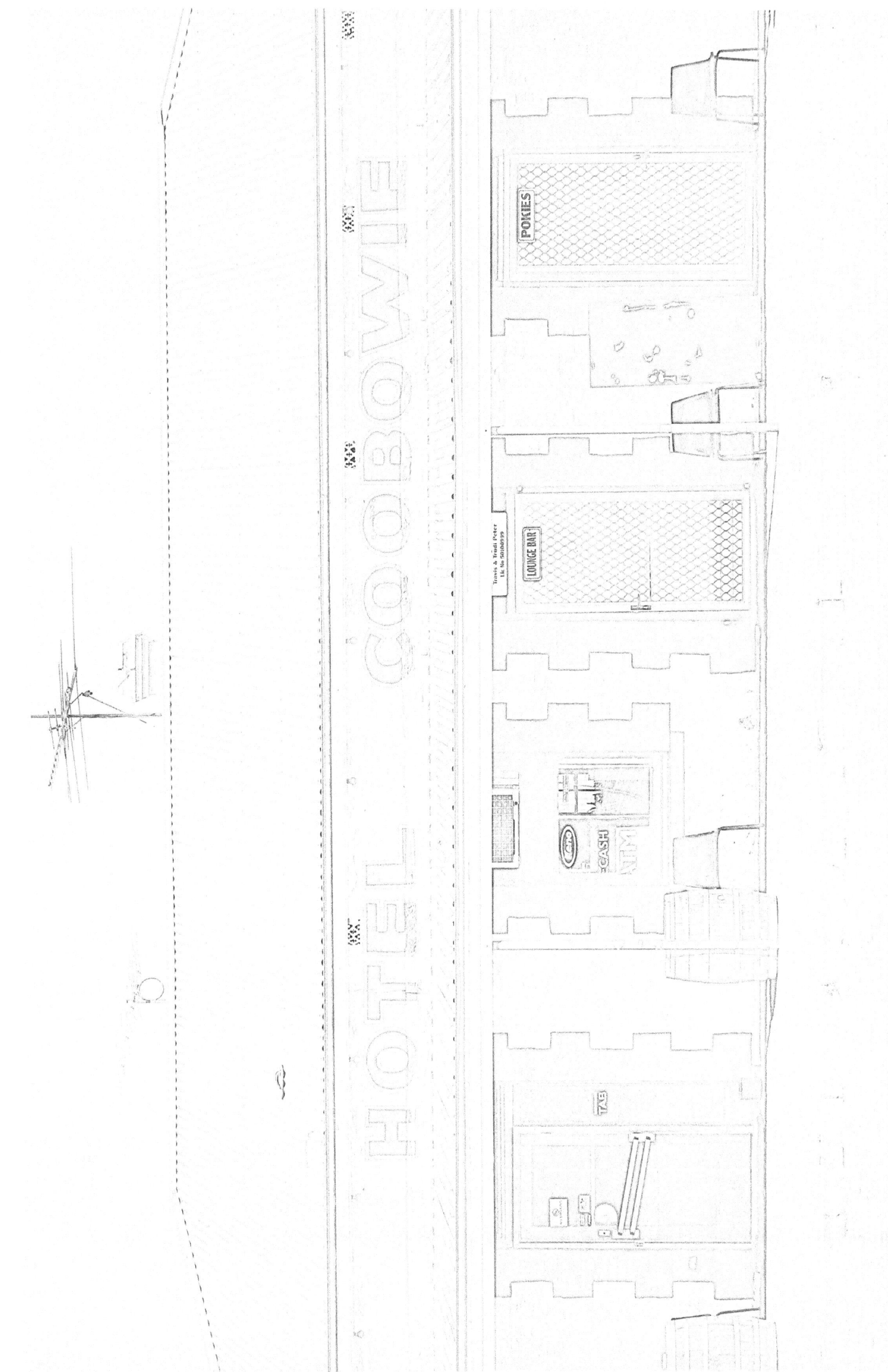

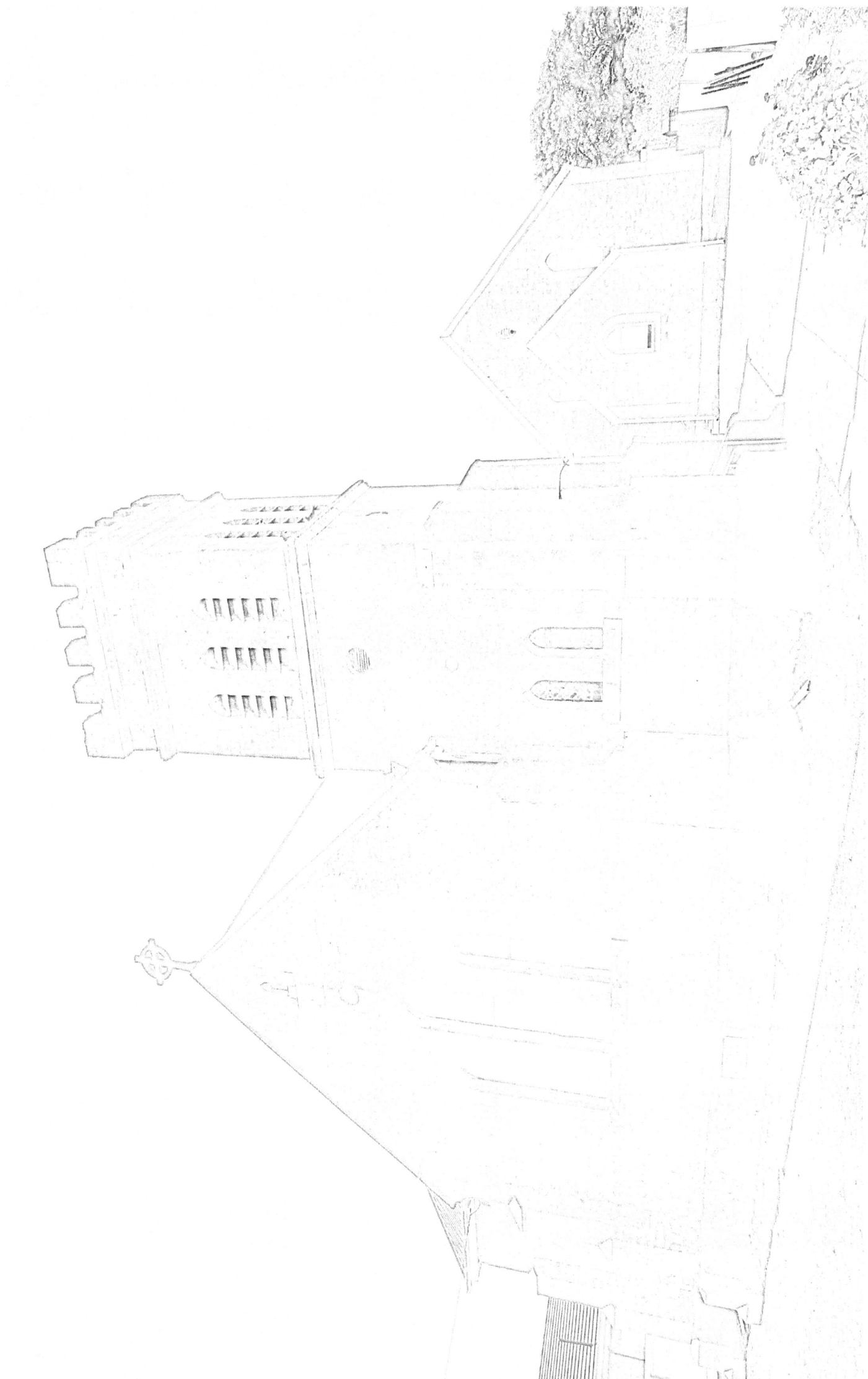

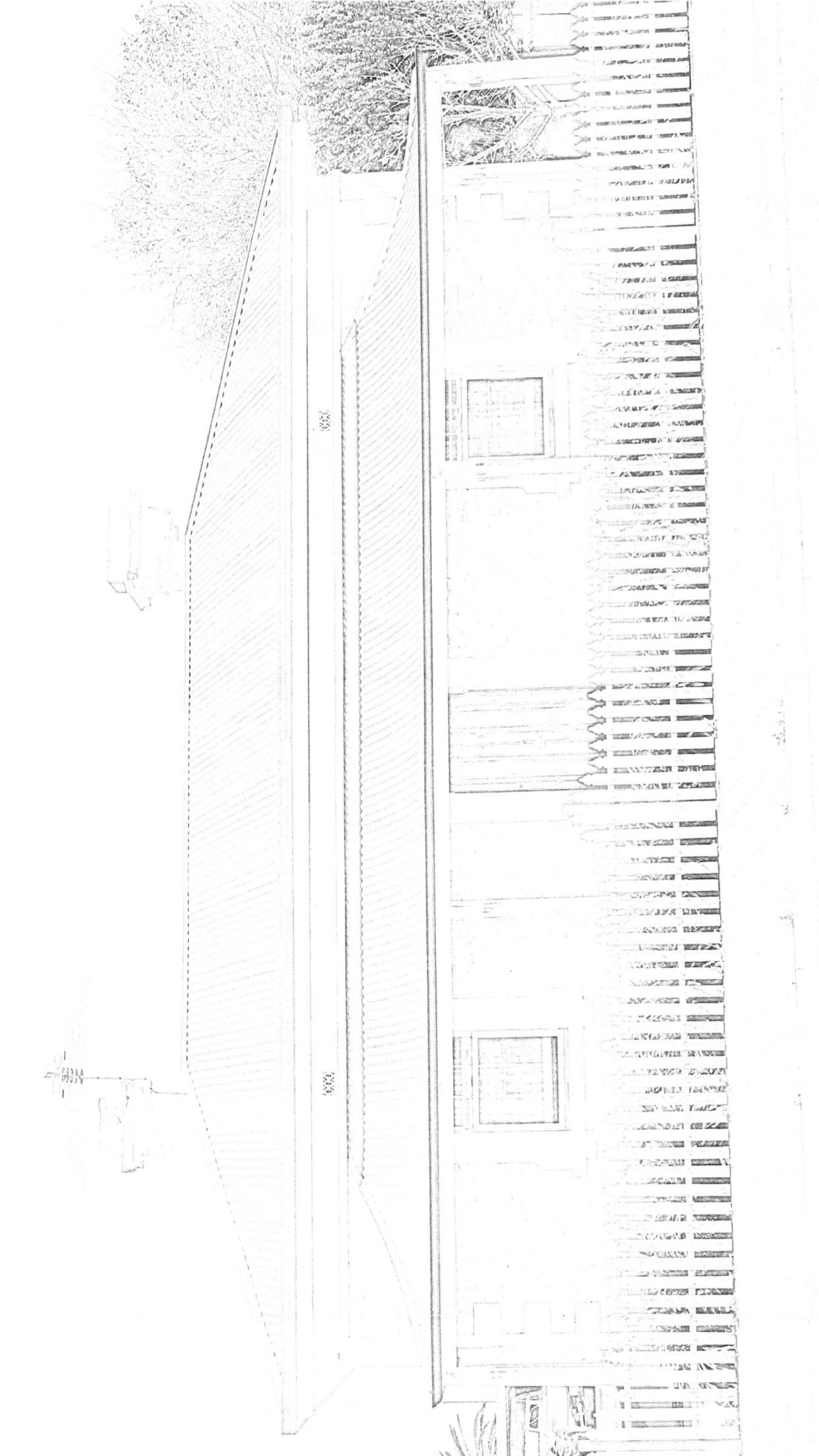

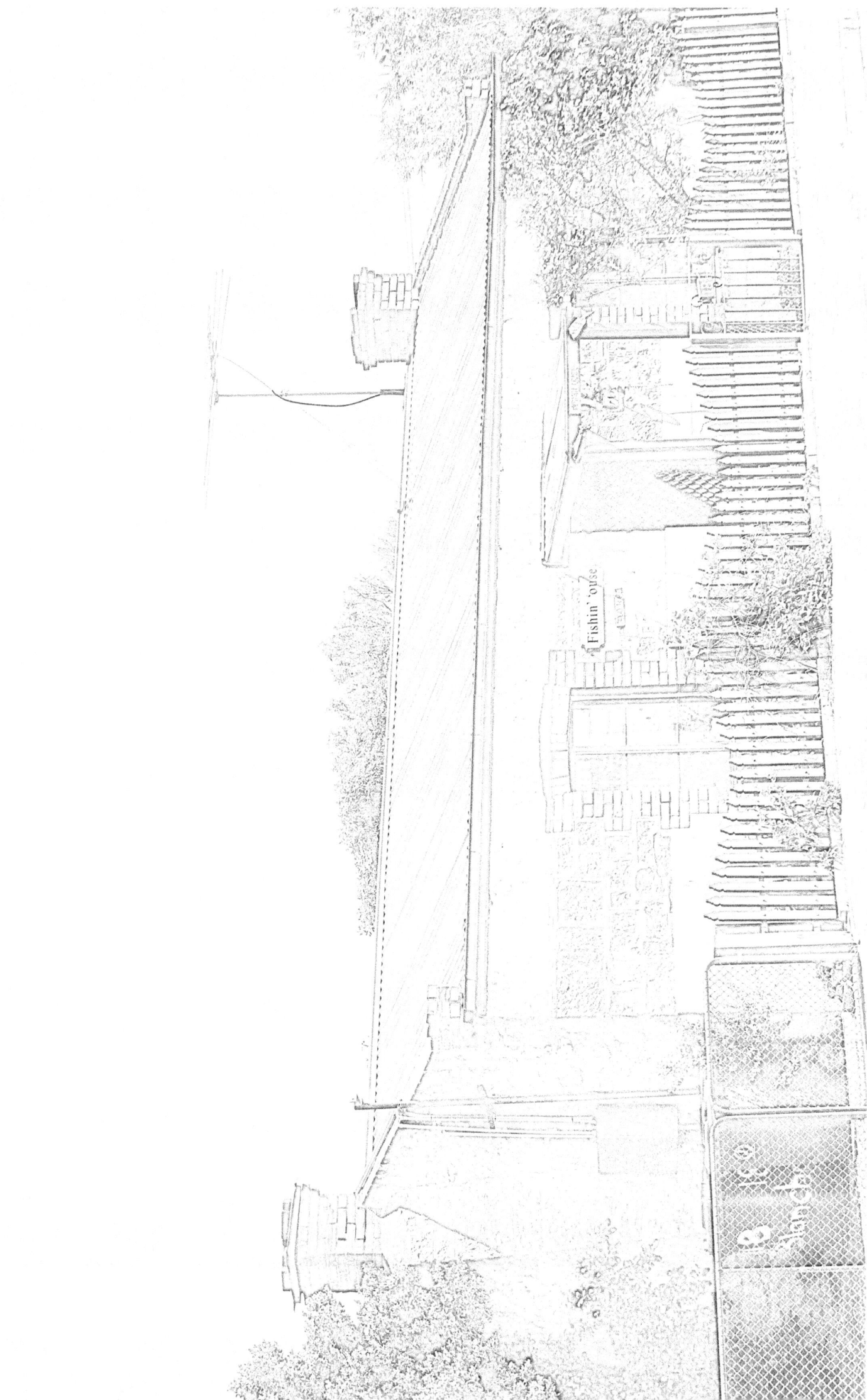

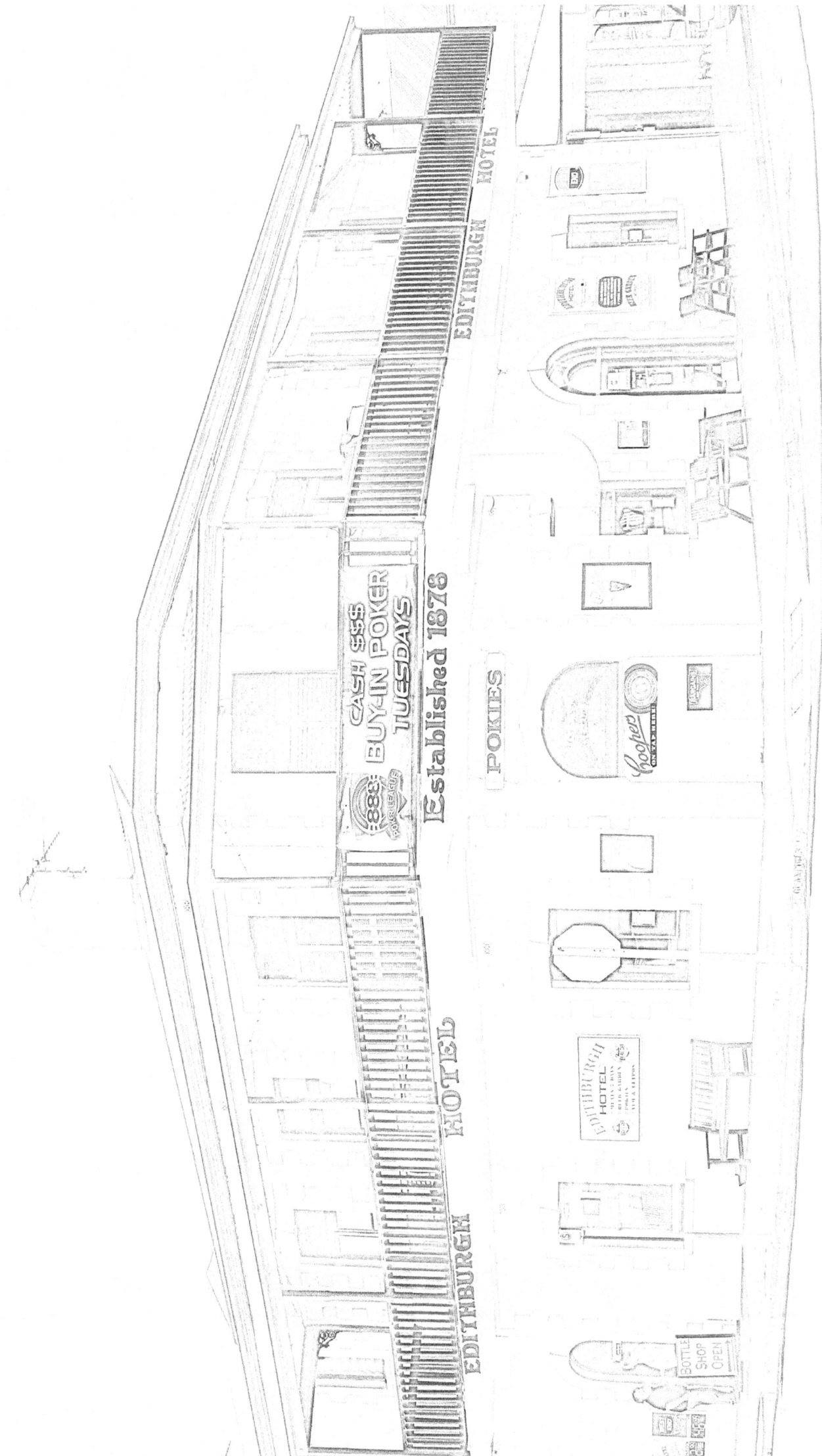

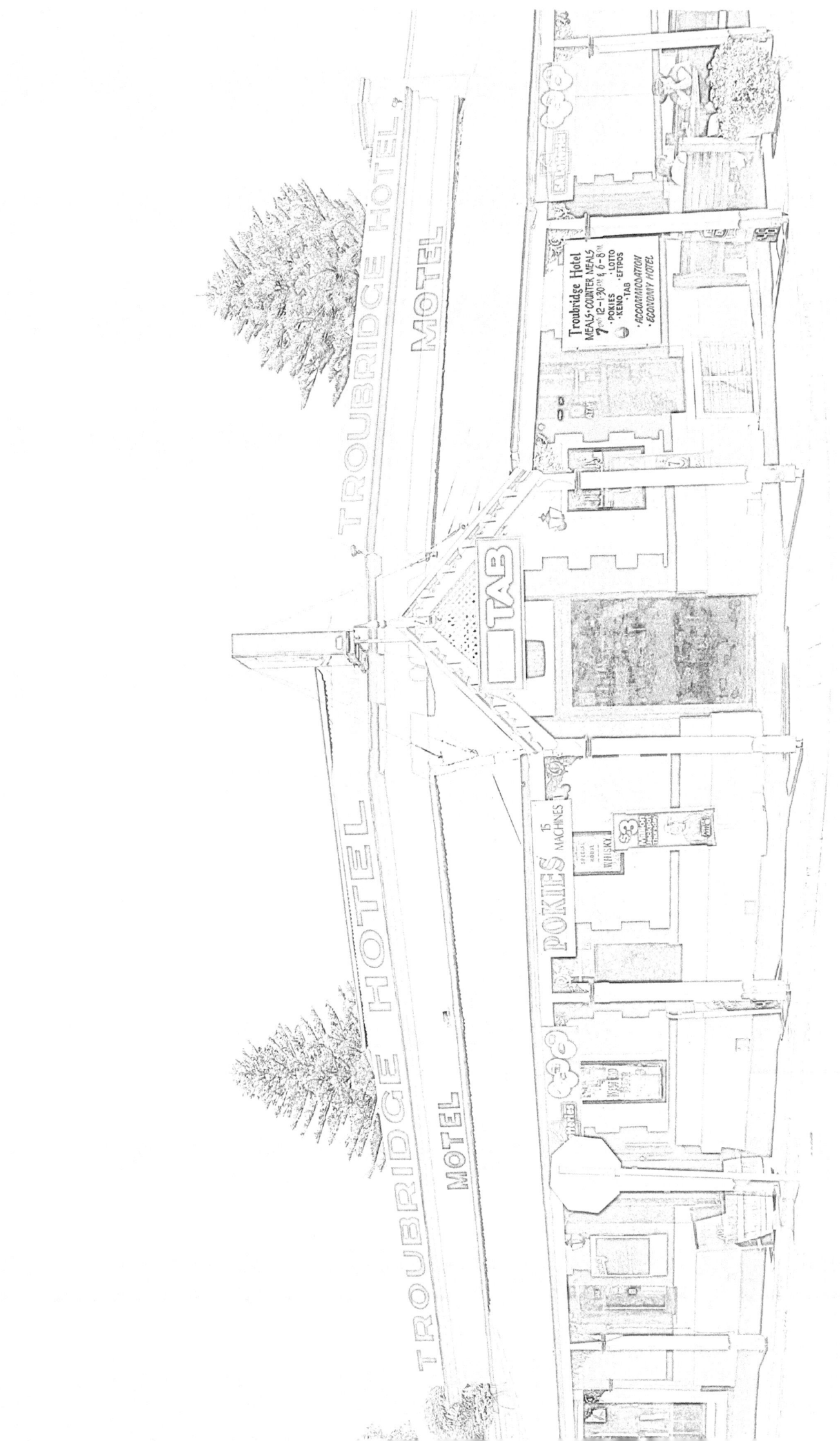

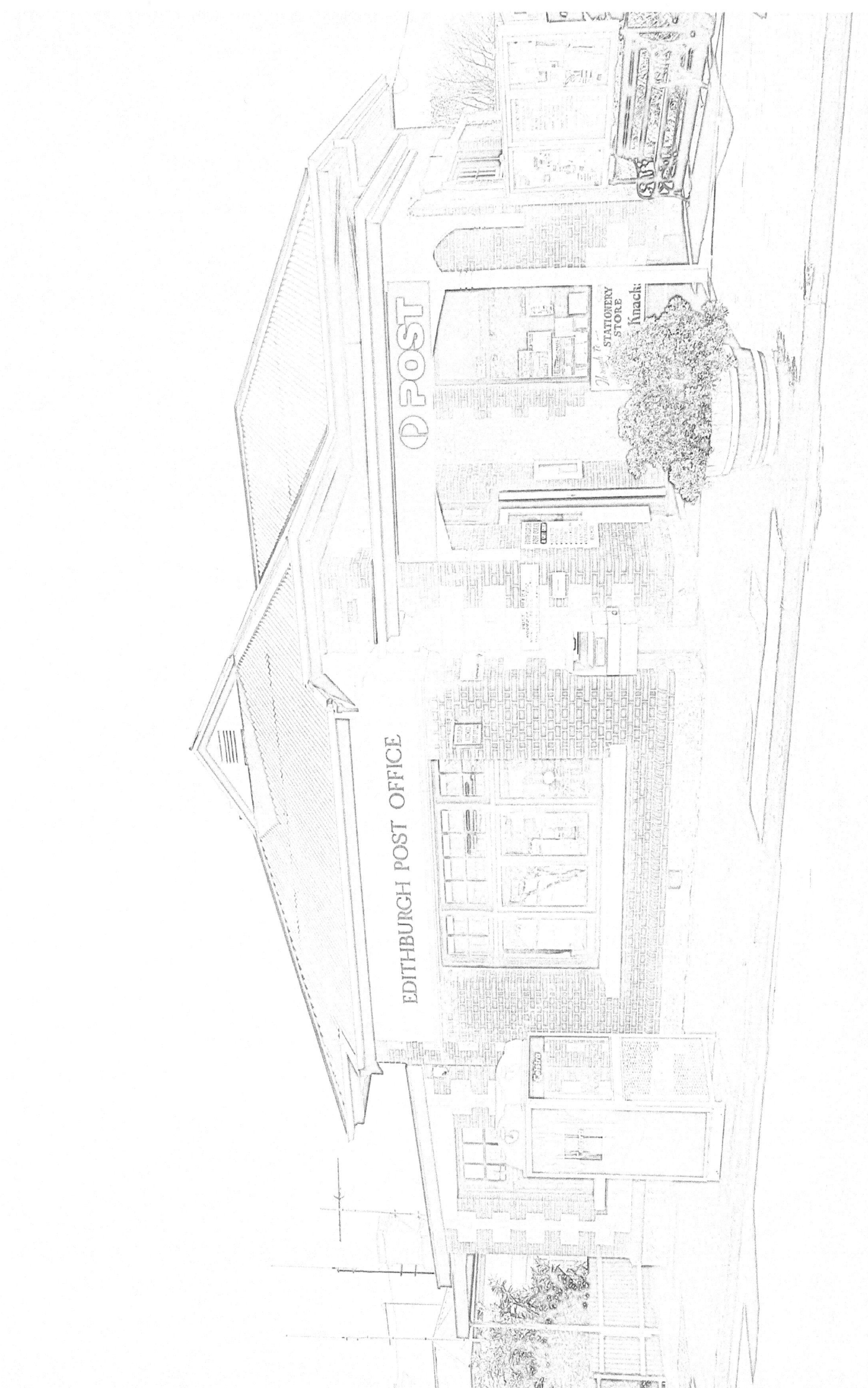

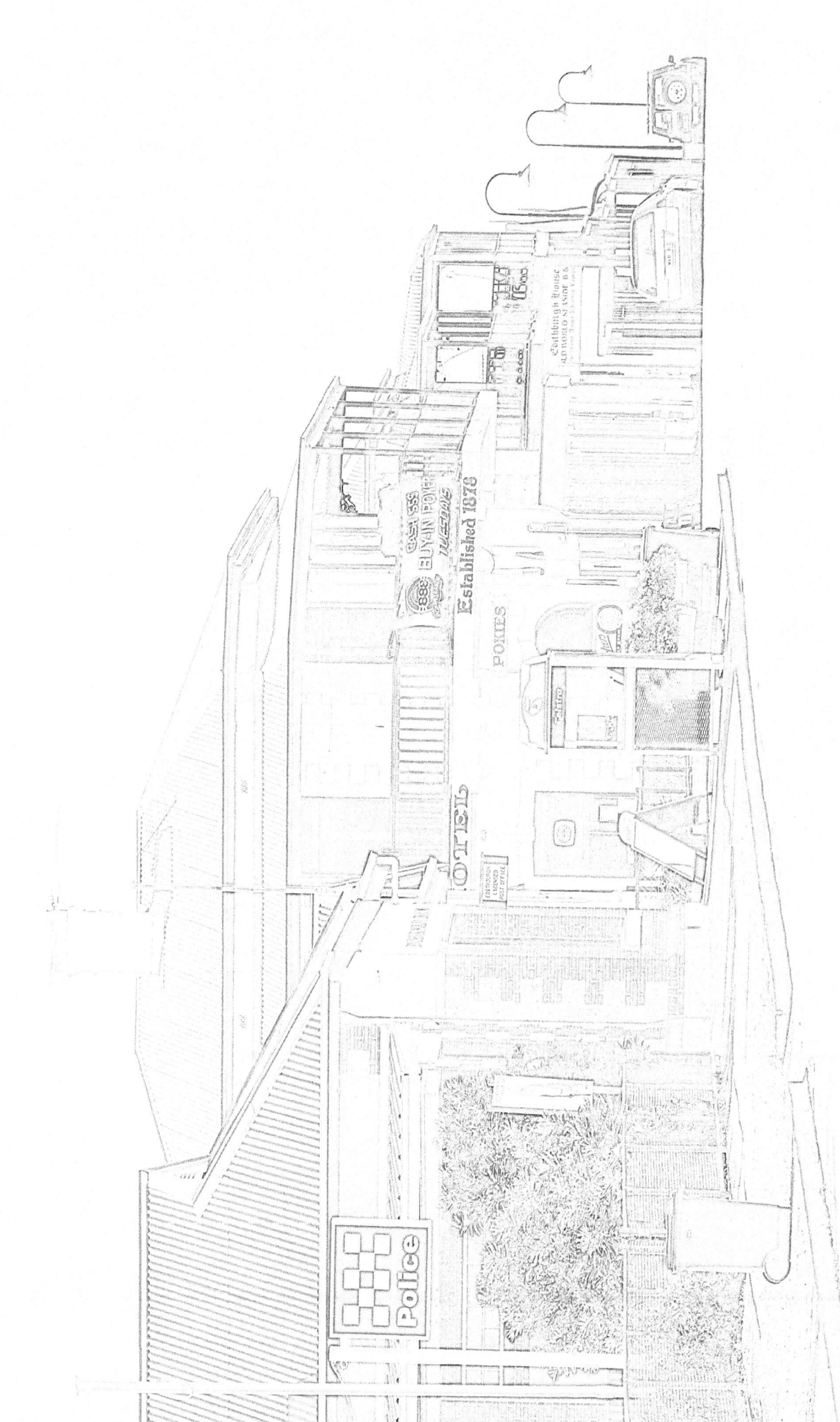

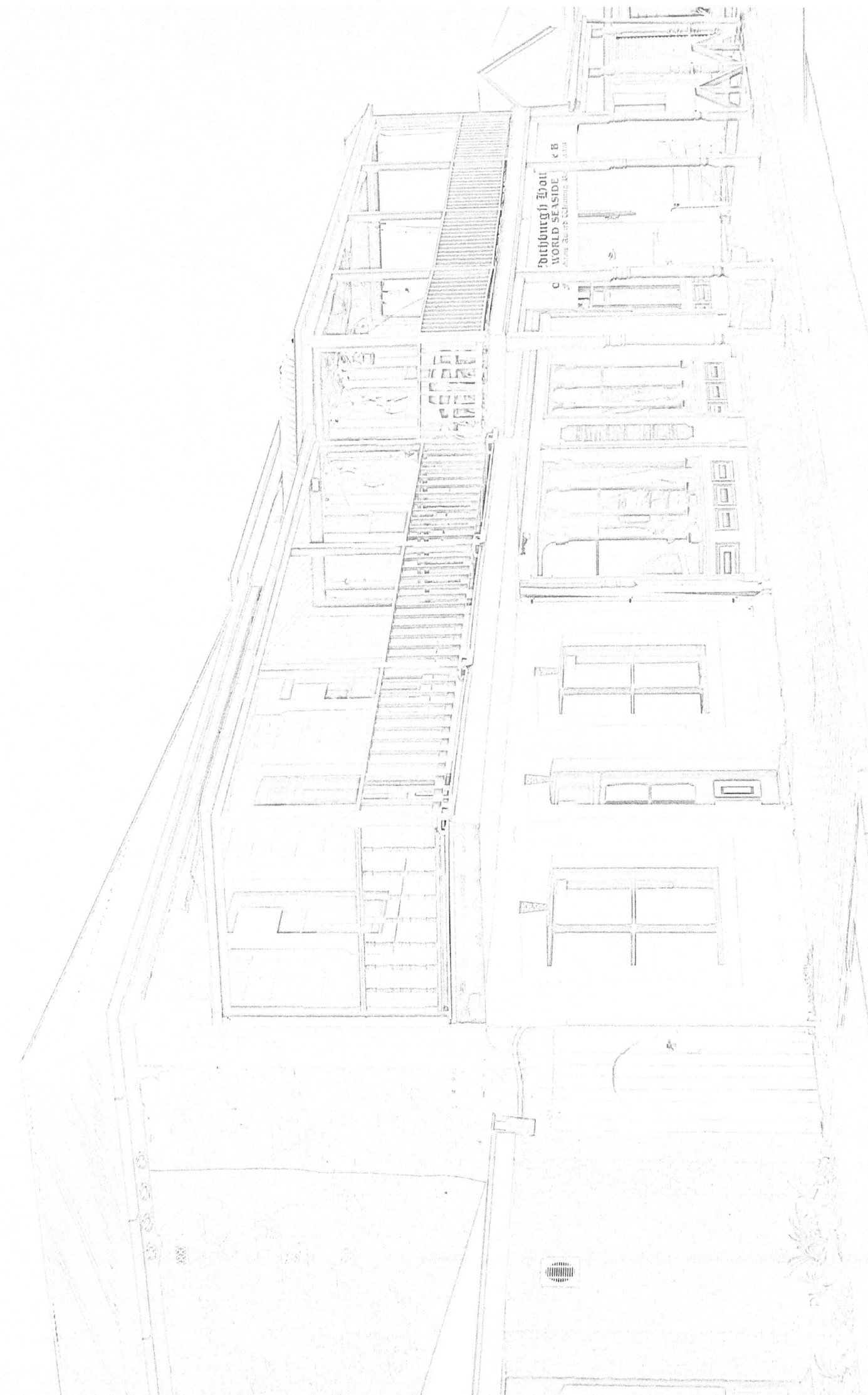

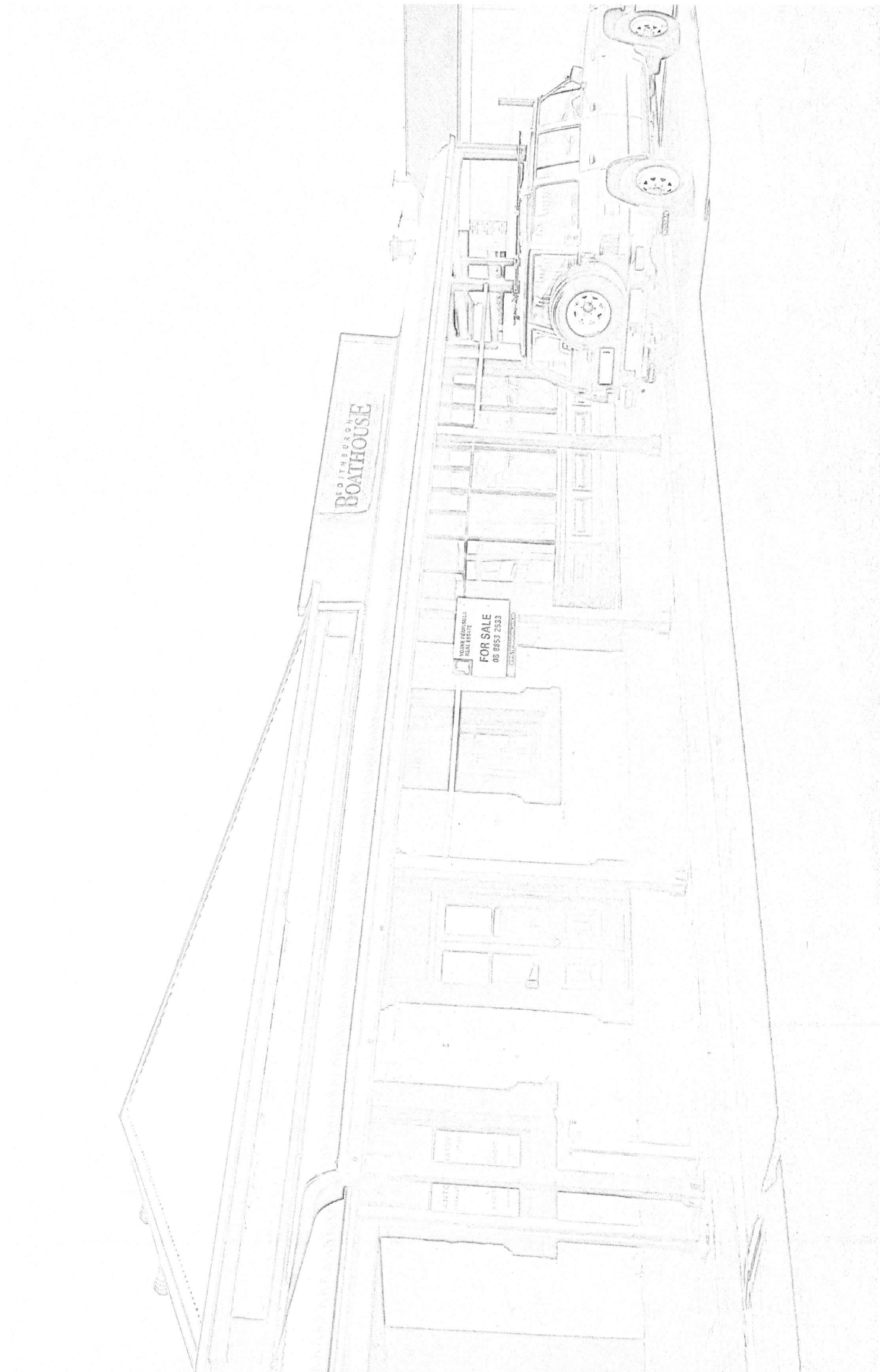

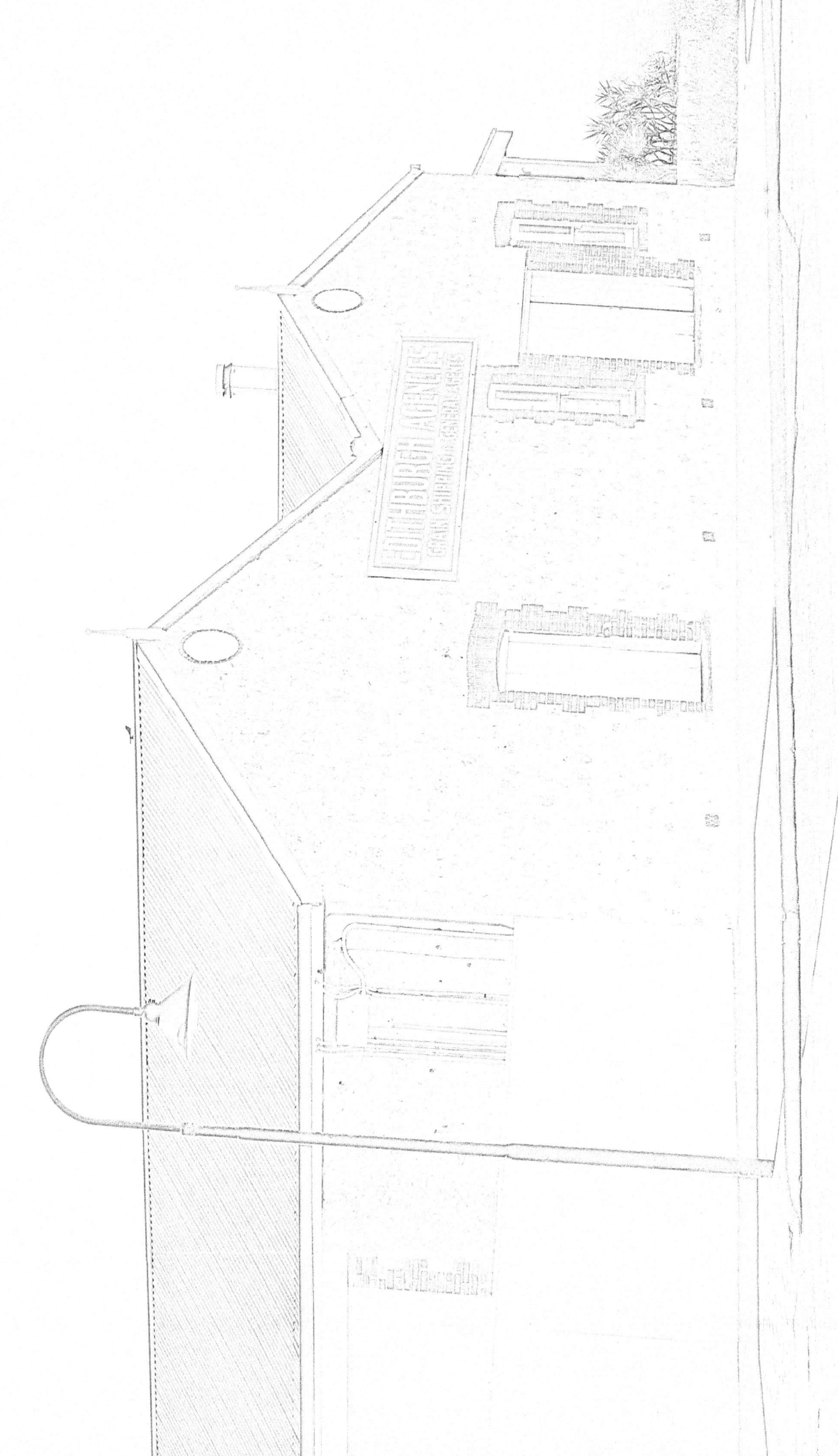

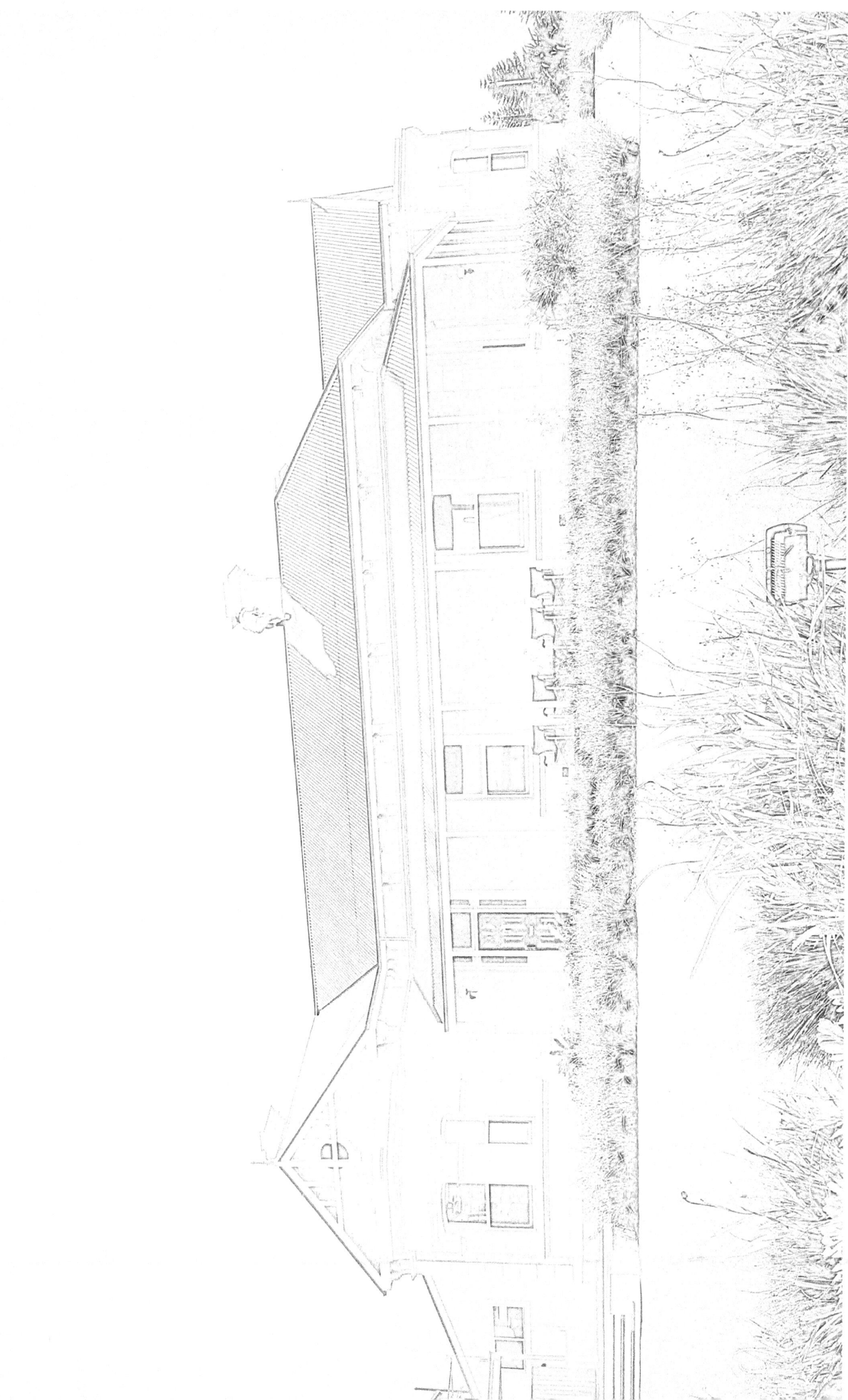

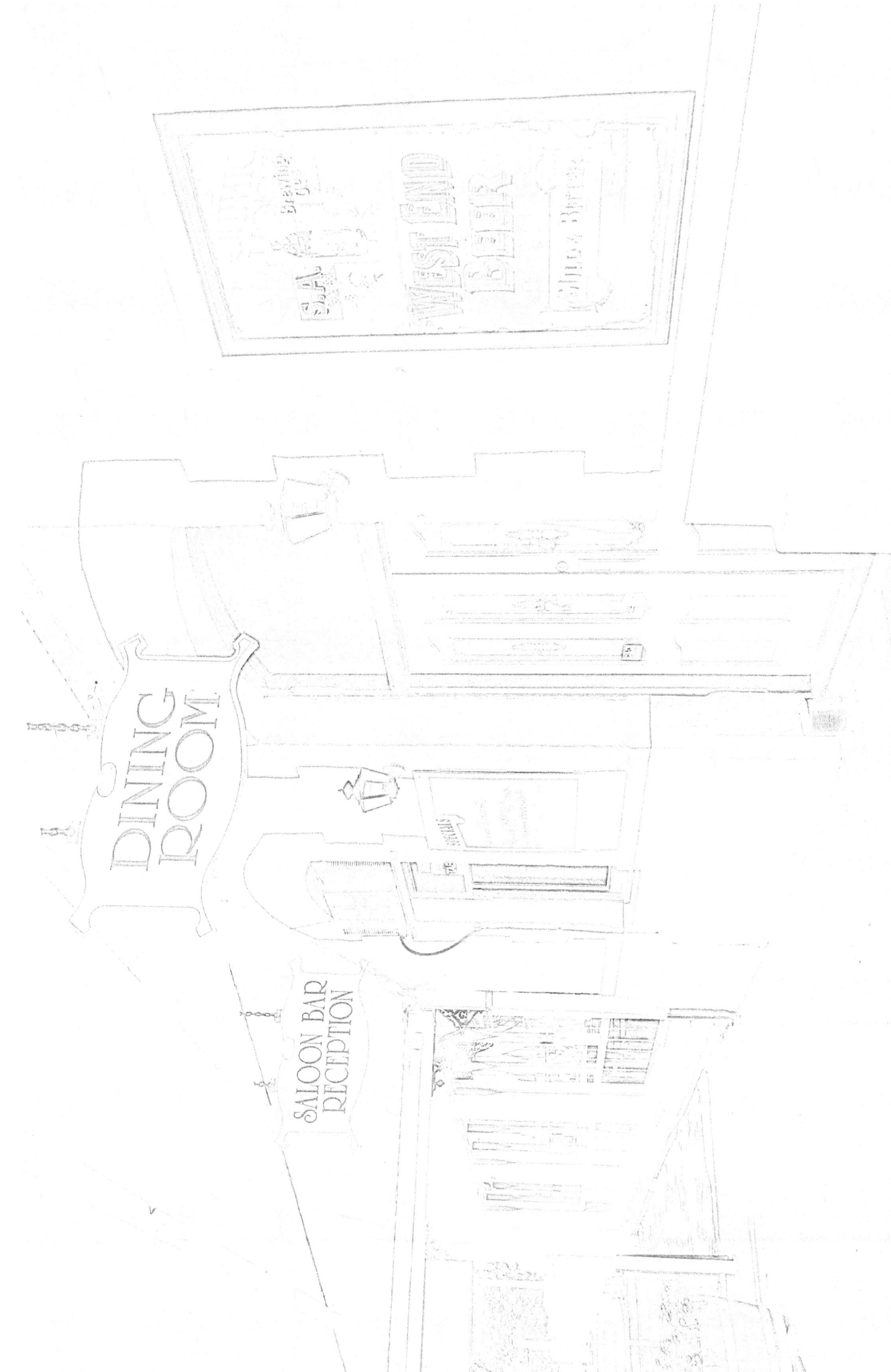

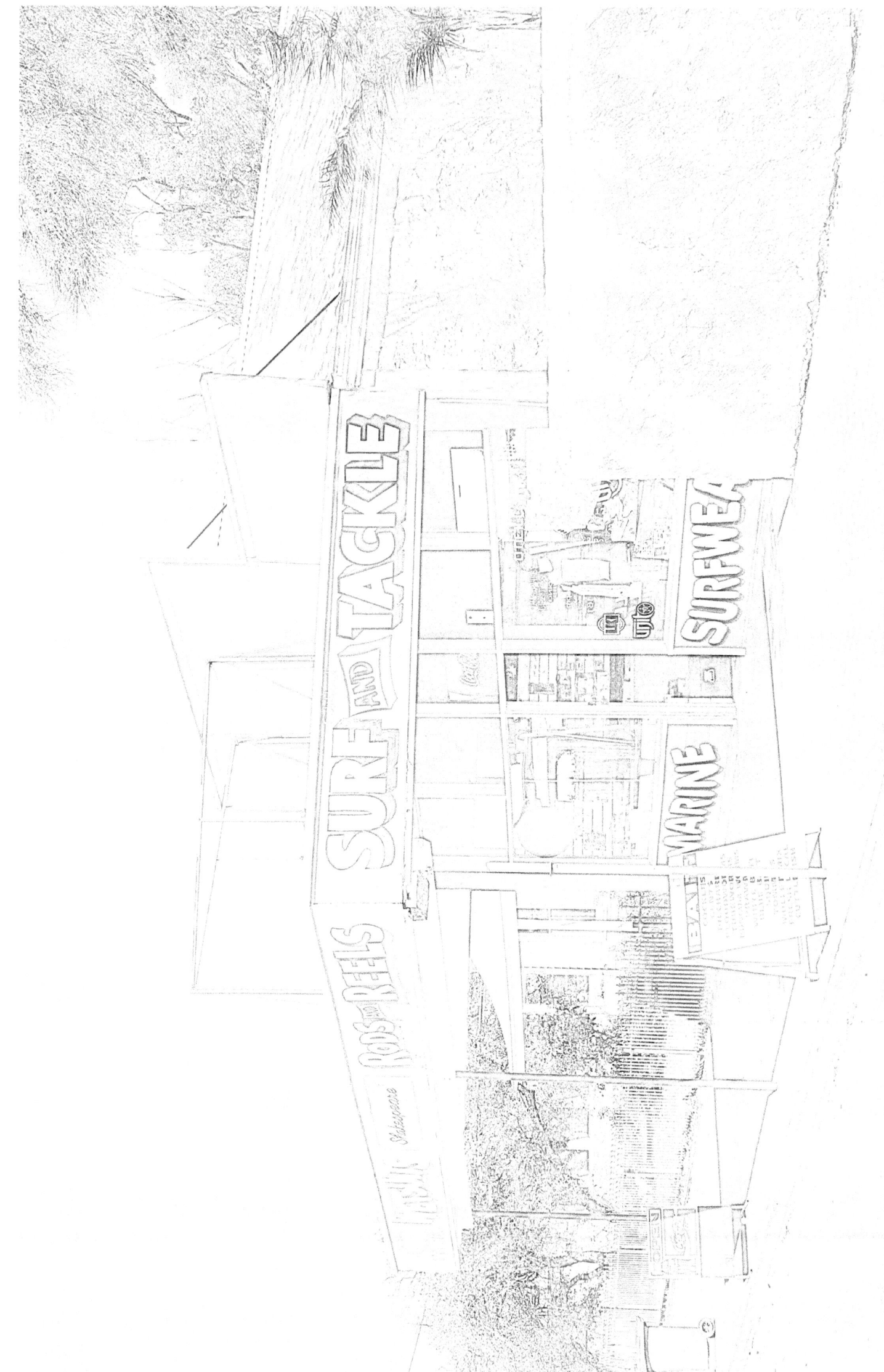

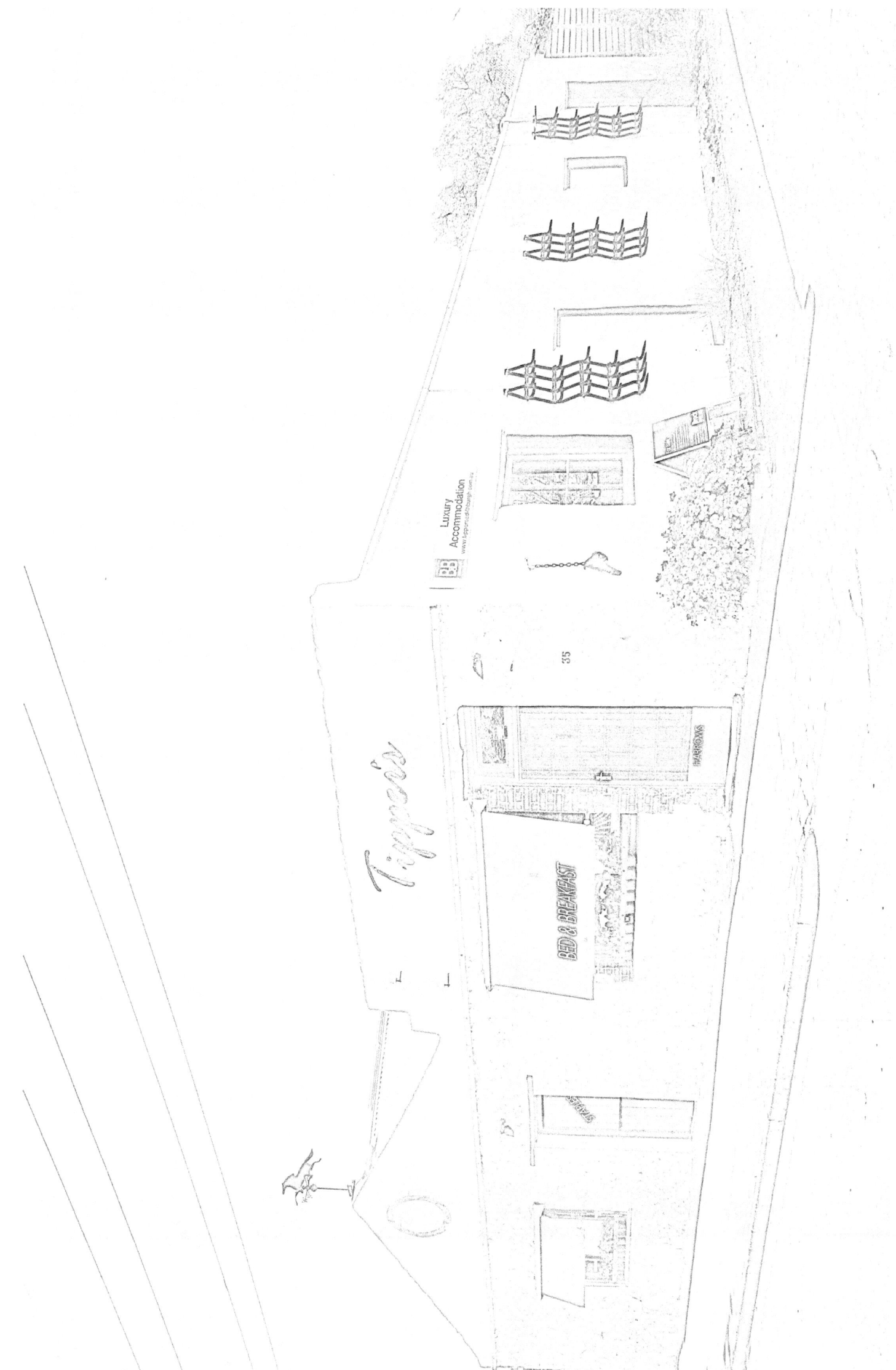

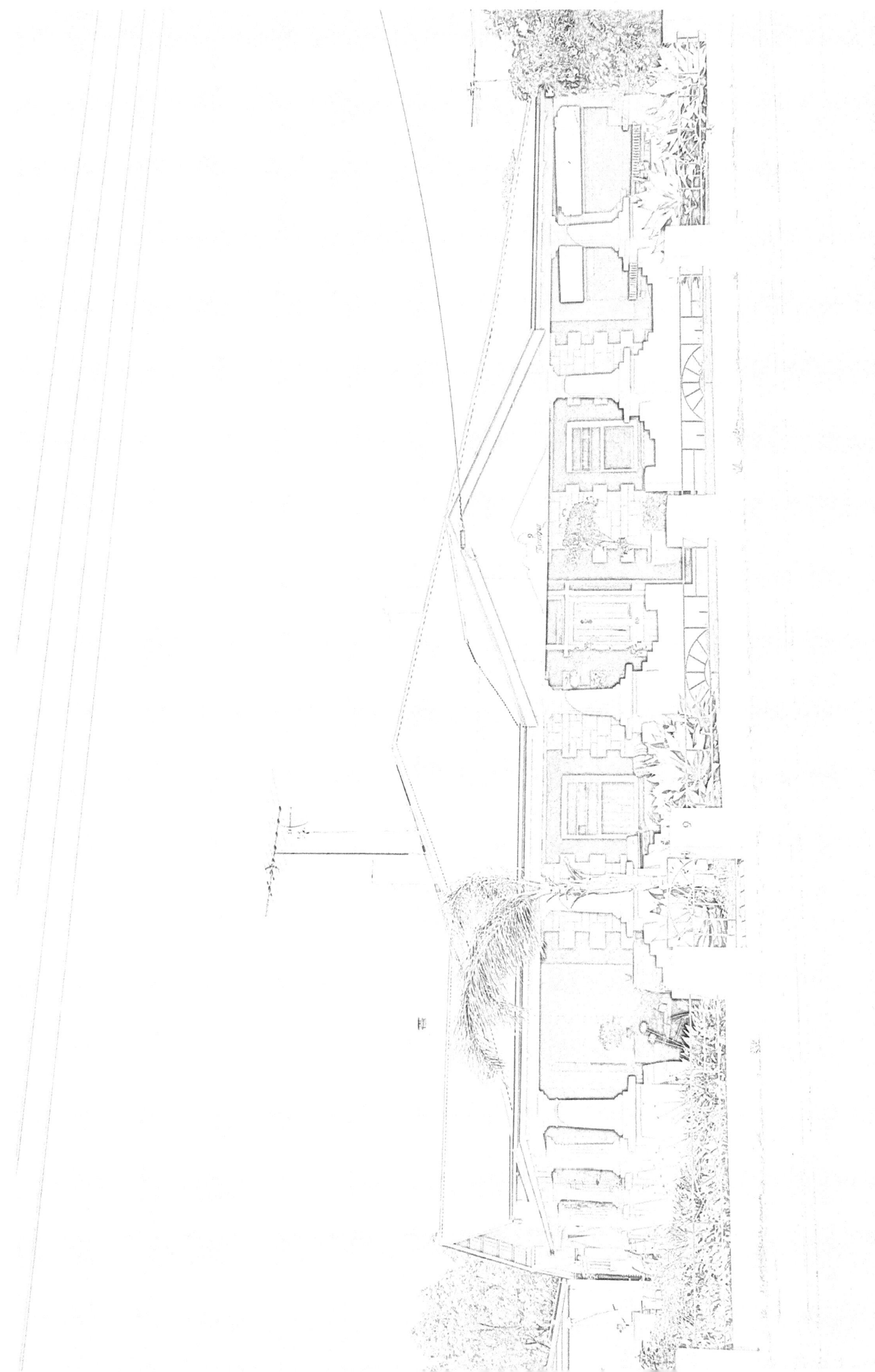

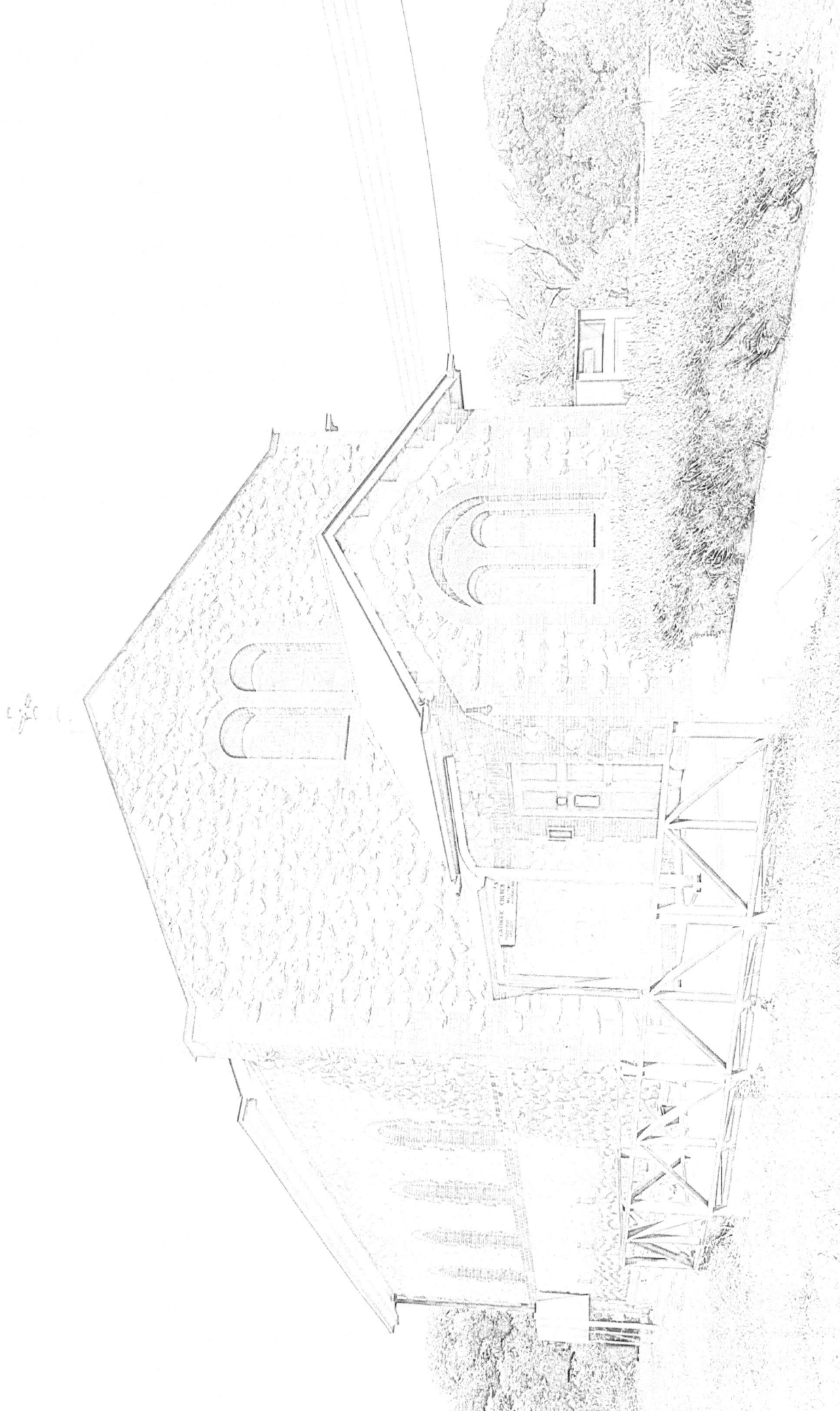

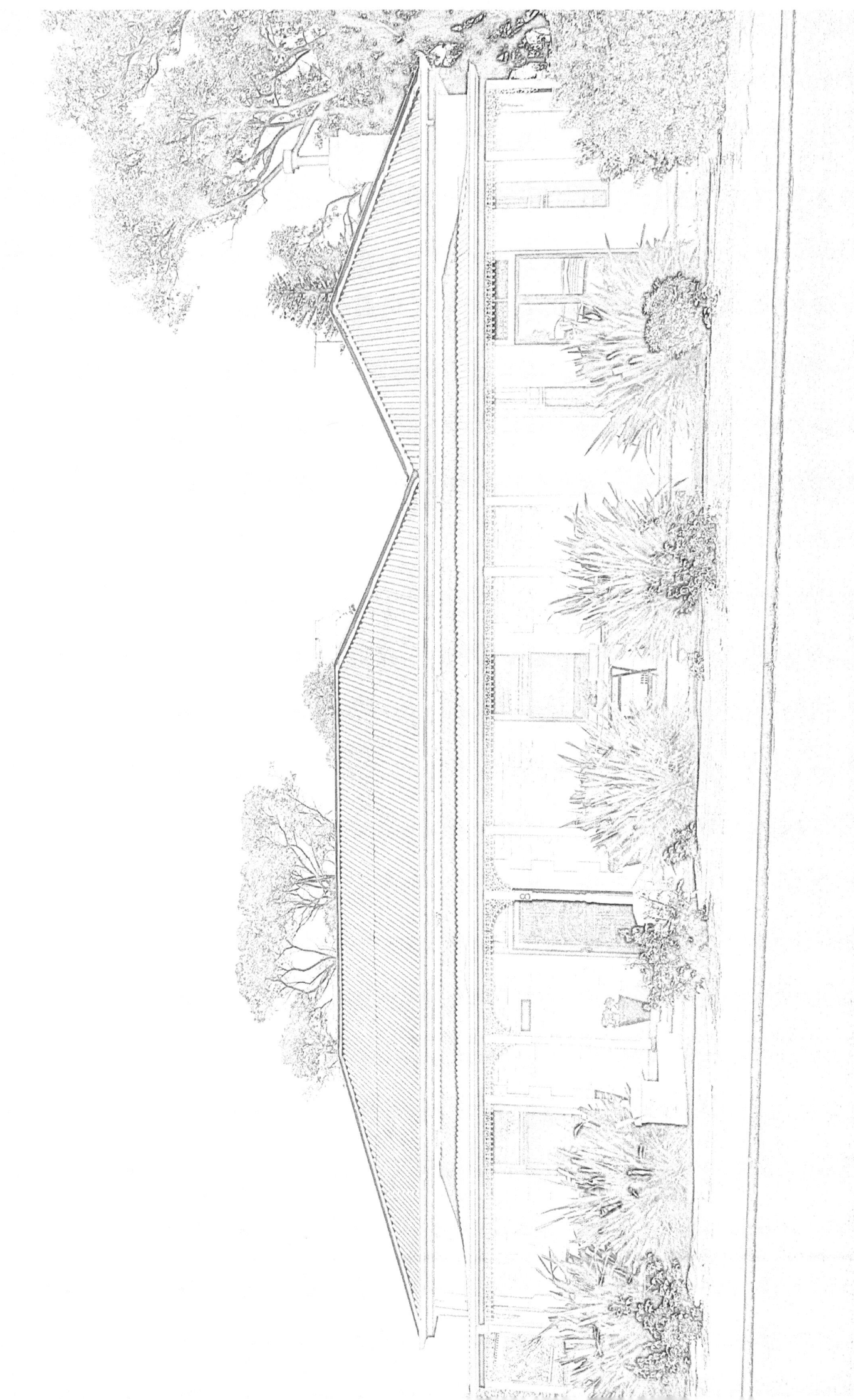

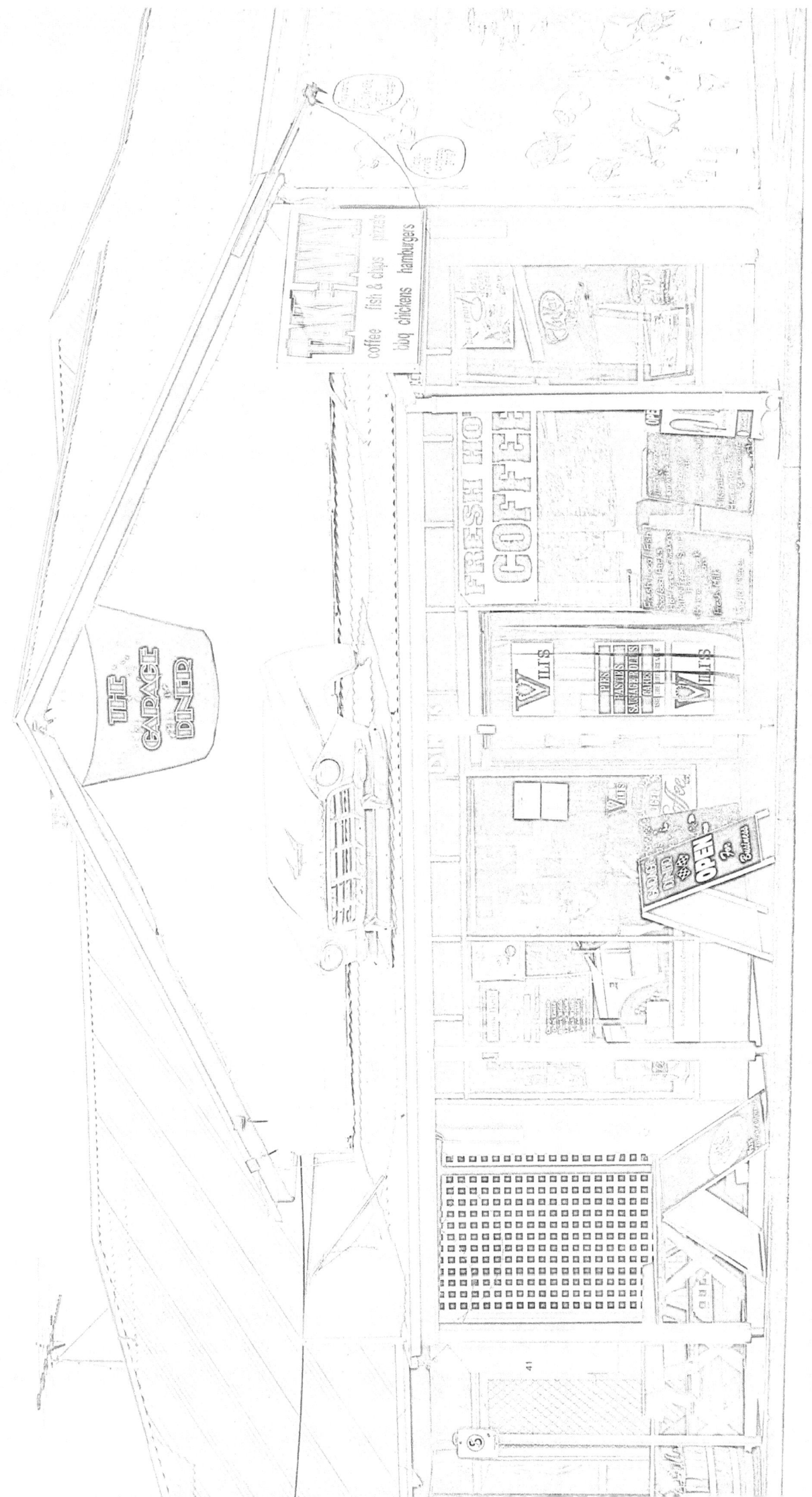

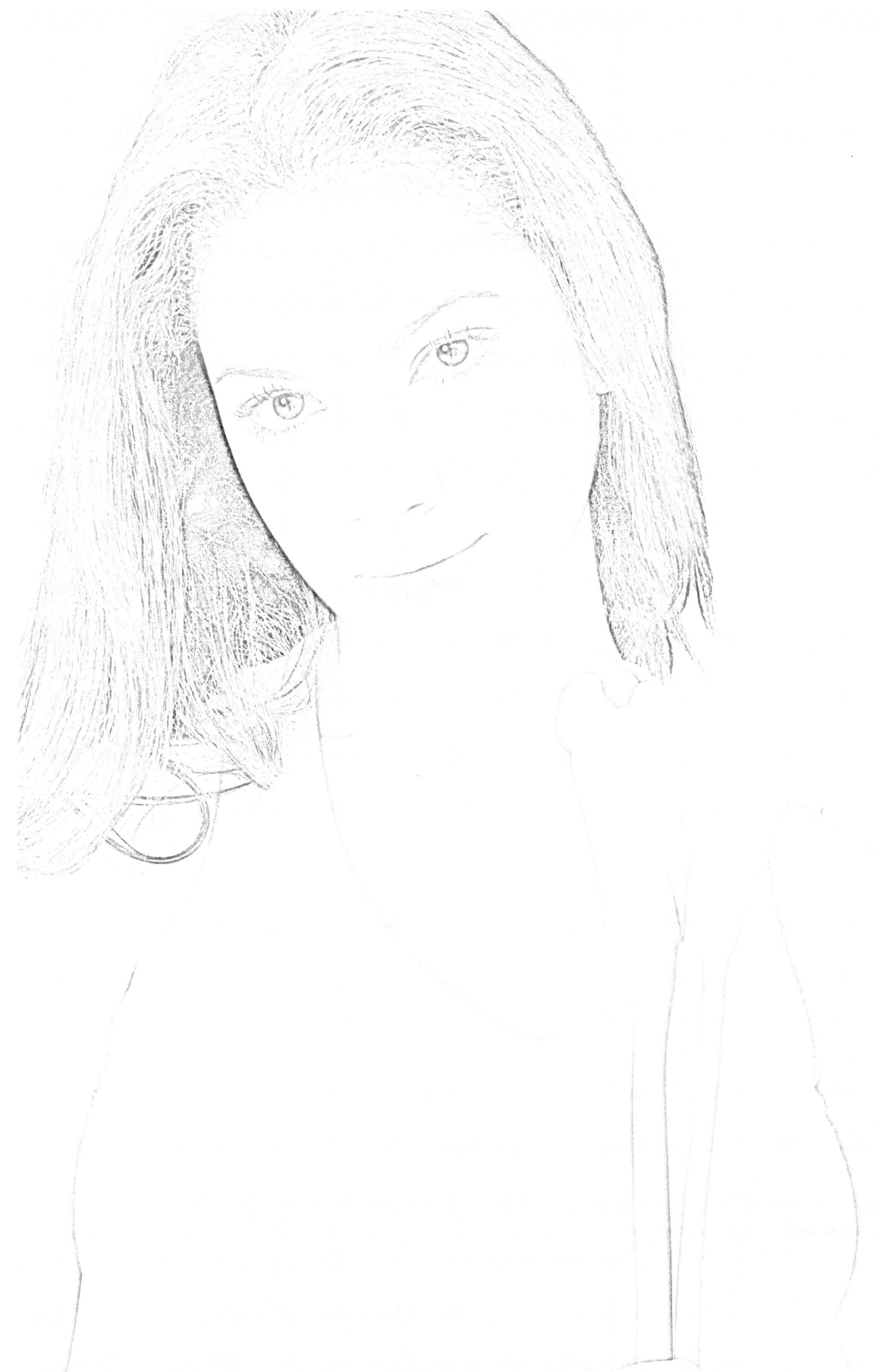

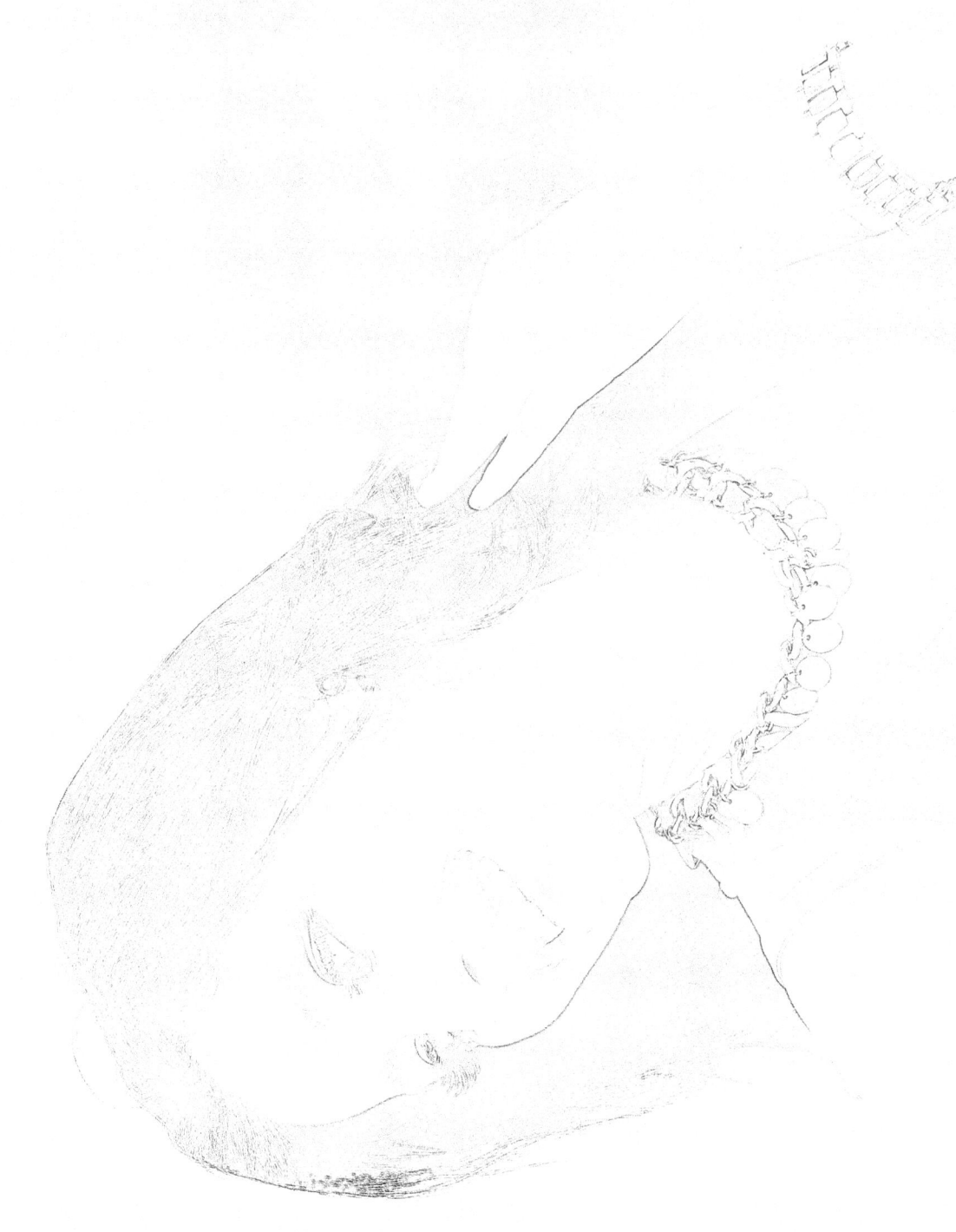